When should the invitations be mailed?

Should the bride ever wear black?

What is the correct form for newspaper announcements?

What should you do if gifts arrive broken?

Can you ever issue invitations by phone?

Should you send wedding invitations to out-of-town friends even though you know they can't come?

What is the proper form for "Thank you" notes?

What are the responsibilities of the groom's parents?

In a double-ring ceremony, who is responsible for the groom's ring?

When do you use pew cards for a church wedding?

When is the wedding cake cut?

YOU AND YOUR WEDDING

EVERYTHING THE BRIDE AND GROOM NEED TO KNOW FOR A PERFECT WEDDING

You and Your Wedding

By Winifred Gray

Illustrations by DAVID NASH

BANTAM BOOKS · TORONTO · NEW YORK · LONDON

YOU AND YOUR WEDDING

A Bantam Book / published April 1965

2nd printing .... *April 1965*		*6th printing* ...... *August 1968*
3rd printing .... *May 1965*		*7th printing* .... *April 1969*
4th printing .... *May 1967*		*8th printing* .... *December 1969*
5th printing ... *December 1967*		*9th printing* .... *May 1970*

10th printing

11th printing

12th printing

13th printing

14th printing

15th printing

16th printing

Published simultaneously in the United States and Canada

Bantam Books are published by Bantam Books, Inc., a National
General company. Its trade-mark, consisting of the words "Bantam
Books" and the portrayal of a bantam, is registered in the United
States Patent Office and in other countries. Marca Registrada.
Bantam Books, Inc., 666 Fifth Avenue, New York, N.Y. 10019.

PRINTED IN THE UNITED STATES OF AMERICA

ACKNOWLEDGMENTS

To Dorothy Melrose who edited laboriously and happily from the rough drafts to the galley proofs.

To Dr. Rickett who so graciously gave his time to assist with the editing.

To my Father whose belief in me gave me the incentive to start *You and Your Wedding*.

To Sara Jones who through experience with her beautiful shop, The Home and Hobby House, made me cognizant of the many perplexing problems facing the bride-to-be and her mother, the answers to which may be found in *You and Your Wedding*.

To Daisy who intuitively assumed household responsibilities, giving me added hours to devote to *You and Your Wedding*.

AUTHOR'S NOTE

Different Locations—Different Customs

Location plays a very important role in the interpretation of the degree of the formality of a wedding. For instance a wedding that is considered very formal in the South and West takes on a semi-formal appearance in the East. Even though many weddings are held at night in the more casual South and West, the male participants do not feel it necessary to wear full evening attire. Although the formality of the wedding is determined by the type of wedding gown worn by the bride, at Southern and Western weddings the bride wears a formal wedding gown with full sweeping train and veil, while the men elect to dress in dinner jackets (summer or winter) instead of full evening dress.

This trend has not come about because society as a whole in these locations is unaware of the correct male attire for a formal wedding, but because living has assumed a more casual trend in these areas. The dinner jacket is worn to so many evening functions that everyone seems to possess this attire and thus an additional expense to an attendant is avoided.

While in large cities, especially Eastern ones, full evening attire is easily rented, in other areas this is not the case; thus the considerate groom may hesitate to ask his attendants to buy full evening dress for this one occasion.

The serving of refreshments also varies. In many locations the bride's table is considered essential at the ultra-formal or formal reception. In other areas, even at the most formal reception, guests are served buffet style without a special table for the bridal party.

There are other variations, some of which are mentioned in following chapters. There are many communities that have set up their own particular customs. Brides in these areas will be aware of them; others need not be informed.

CONTENTS

tions • When the Groom's Family Gives the Wedding • Invitations That Require an Answer • Church Wedding • Wedding Anniversary Invitations • The Bride Issues Her Own Invitations • Double Weddings • Home Weddings • Invitation for Adopted Daughter • Wedding Invitation of the Young Widow • Mature Widow's Invitation • The Mature Bride • Overseas Bride • Invitation of the Young Divorcee • Invitation of the Older Divorcee • The Remarriage of Divorced Persons to Each Other • Emergencies • Returning Wedding Gifts • Handwritten Informal Invitations • Telephoned Invitations

Chapter 1. The Newspaper Publicity

ENGAGEMENT ANNOUNCEMENT *NO*

Engagements are announced in the newspaper by the parents of the bride or, if both parents are deceased, by a close relative, a guardian, or a friend. See pages 4-5.

In a small community where a family (or families) is well known to the society editor, very little information other than names, dates, etc., need be volunteered; many times this information is telephoned to her. In a larger city, unless the families are very prominent, the announcement should be accompanied by some other newsworthy material, such as names of both sets of grandparents, schools attended by both the bride and the groom, military service, position held by groom, etc. All information is *written* on a sheet of white paper and either mailed or taken to the newspaper office or the society editor. All names, schools, dates, and addresses must be spelled correctly.

Since unidentified stories are often discarded by editors, the name of the bride's mother (father, guardian, a relative, or friend) with her telephone number and address is placed in the upper right-hand corner of the copy. That person also acts as spokesman for any additional information that may be required.

Some newspapers have regular forms to fill out for engagement announcements, weddings, parties, etc. These forms will be mailed upon request. The following sample form is similar to that used by most newspapers:

Name of the bride in full (no initials)
Home address
Telephone number
Name and residence of the bride's parents
Name and residence of the groom
Name and residence of the groom's parents
Date, place, and hour of the ceremony
Name of the officiating minister
Name of person giving bride in marriage
Description of bride's dress, veil, and flowers
Maid (or matron) of honor
Bridesmaids
Description of dresses and flowers of bride's attendants
Best man
Names and residences of groom's attendants
Time and place of the reception
Wedding trip
New residence

RELEASE DATE

Copy to the newspaper must be marked very clearly with the release date:

Release Date: Tuesday, April 5

Marking the copy with the release date is very important, especially if the announcement is a surprise or if the engagement is to be announced with a surprise party.

PICTURE

If a picture is to be used with the announcement, the newspaper should be contacted to learn what its procedure is. Many newspapers have their own staff photographers and only their photographs are used; others accept pictures made by outside photographers. If a picture is being sent with the announcement copy, no information should be written upon the back of the picture. A typewritten or clearly handwritten sheet of paper is attached to the picture with all information, such as:

Miss Dorothy Waters,* whose engagement is to be announced Tuesday, April 24.

* Through necessity a wide variety of names has been used. If any name is that of a real person, living or dead, it is a coincidence.

The picture is clipped to the newspaper copy and mailed or taken to the newspaper office.

If the groom's parents live in another city, a duplicate copy of the announcement, with or without picture, is sent to them or to their newspaper.

NEWSPAPER ENGAGEMENT ANNOUNCEMENT

Release date	Mrs. Clarence A. Lloyd (mother)
Monday, June 10	246 Spring Dr., Jacksonville
	Telephone: CApital 5672

Mr. and Mrs. Clarence Atwood Lloyd, of 246 Spring Drive, announce the engagement of their daughter, Beverly Anne, to Mr. Richard Yates, son of Mr. and Mrs. Marshall Yates, of Miami, Florida.

Miss Lloyd is a graduate of Stephens College, Columbia, Missouri, and of the University of Florida. Mr. Yates attended the Citadel prior to entering the Army and serving in Korea. He was graduated from the University of Florida where he was a member of Florida Blue Key honorary fraternity and Alpha Omega. He is now practicing law in Jacksonville. The wedding will take place in August.

ENGAGEMENT ANNOUNCED WITH PARTY

If a party is being given to announce the engagement, all party information is written out and the same procedure as that for announcing engagements is followed for its release.

DETAILS OF THE WEDDING

Details of the wedding are written out in much the same way as the engagement details, marked clearly with the RELEASE DATE and time.

Wedding information should be sent or taken to the newspaper office four or five days before the ceremony.

All names, dates, schools, cities, etc., must be spelled correctly.

WEDDING ANNOUNCEMENT

An announcement of a marriage that has already taken place should be sent or taken to the newspaper immediately after the marriage. (Wording for special cases is discussed later in the chapter.)

DECEASED PARENTS

The word "late" should precede any reference made to a deceased parent. There are two exceptions as noted under *Mother deceased—Father remarried*.

FATHER DECEASED—MOTHER NOT REMARRIED

. . . daughter of Mrs. Clarence Atwood Lloyd and the late Mr. Lloyd.

. . . son of Mrs. Marshall Yates and the late Mr. Yates.

FATHER DECEASED—MOTHER REMARRIED

Mr. and Mrs. Harold Deems Tindall, Iowa City, Iowa, announce the marriage (or engagement) of Mrs. Tindall's daughter, Beverly Anne Lloyd, to, etc.

. . . Miss Lloyd is the daughter of the late Mr. Clarence Atwood Lloyd.

or:

. . . Mr. Yates is the son of Mrs. David Parks Weeks and the late Mr. Marshall Yates.

MOTHER DECEASED—FATHER NOT REMARRIED

. . . daughter of Mr. Clarence Atwood Lloyd and the late Mrs. Lloyd.

. . . son of Mr. Marshall Yates and the late Mrs. Yates.

MOTHER DECEASED—FATHER REMARRIED

Here no mention of the late need be made as it is apparent.

Mr. Clarence Atwood Lloyd announces the engagement (or marriage) of his daughter, Beverly Anne, to, etc.

Or if the father remarried when his daughter was very young and his wife has been the only mother the bride has ever known, the late need not be mentioned.

Mr. and Mrs. Clarence Atwood Lloyd announce the marriage (or engagement) of their daughter, etc.

BOTH PARENTS DECEASED

If both parents are deceased, a close relative makes the announcement.

Mr. and Mrs. Henry Albert Boyd announce the engagement (or marriage) of their granddaughter, Beverly Anne Lloyd, etc.

If the bride has no close relatives, a friend or guardian may make the announcement. If the announcement is made by a close relative (sister, brother, aunt, uncle, grandparents), the relationship is noted. The connection is not shown if the announcement is made by friends, cousins, guardian, etc. In some cases the bride and groom may announce their own marriage in the newspaper. See the section, "Principal Making Own Announcement," p. 6.

DIVORCED PARENTS

MOTHER AND FATHER DIVORCED—MOTHER NOT REMARRIED

Mrs. Sutton Lloyd (a combination of the mother's maiden and married surnames) announces the engagement (or marriage) of her daughter Beverly Anne, etc. . . . Miss Lloyd is also the daughter of Mr. Clarence Atwood Lloyd, Chicago.

MOTHER AND FATHER DIVORCED—MOTHER REMARRIED

Mr. and Mrs. Harold Deems Tindall announce the engagement (or marriage) of Mrs. Tindall's daughter, Miss Beverly Anne Lloyd. . . . Miss Lloyd is also the daughter of Mr. Clarence Atwood Lloyd, Chicago.

Or if the bride has known no other father:

Mr. and Mrs. Harold Deems Tindall announce the engagement (or marriage) of their daughter, Miss Beverly Anne Lloyd, etc.

MOTHER AND FATHER DIVORCED—FATHER IS MAKING THE ANNOUNCEMENT

When parents are divorced, the mother usually makes the engagement and marriage newspaper announcement. There are occasions, however, when a father makes the announcement.

FATHER HAS NOT REMARRIED

Mr. Clarence Atwood Lloyd announces the engagement (or marriage) of his daughter, Beverly Anne, etc. . . . Miss Lloyd is also the daughter of Mrs. Sutton Lloyd, Baltimore.

FATHER HAS REMARRIED

Mr. and Mrs. Clarence Atwood Lloyd announce the engagement (or marriage) of his daughter, Beverly Anne, etc. . . . Miss Lloyd is also the daughter of Mrs. Sutton Lloyd, Baltimore.

Or if the bride has known no other mother:

Mr. and Mrs. Clarence Atwood Lloyd announce the engagement (or marriage) of their daughter, Beverly Anne, to, etc.

ENGAGEMENT ANNOUNCED BY BOTH DIVORCED PARENTS

Occasionally an *engagement* is announced in the newspaper by both divorced parents together, even though they have remarried. *Marriages,* however, are never announced this way.

If both divorced parents make the newspaper announcement:

Mrs. Sutton Lloyd (a combination of the mother's maiden and married surnames), Baltimore, Maryland, and Mr. Clarence Atwood Lloyd, Iowa City, Iowa, announce the engagement of their daughter, Beverly Anne, to, etc.

SEPARATED PARENTS

Separated parents issue joint engagement and marriage announcements. A separated mother's name is that of her husband, since she is still married to him.

PRINCIPALS MAKING OWN ANNOUNCEMENT

The mature bride has her choice of letting her parents (if they are still living), a relative, or a friend make her *marriage* announcement; or often she and the groom announce their own marriage.

An *engagement* of the mature bride and groom is not usually formally announced in the newspaper, especially if one (or both) has been married before.

ADOPTED DAUGHTER

If an adopted daughter's name is different from that of her parents:

Mr. and Mrs. William Arthur Andrews announce the engagement (or marriage) of their adopted daughter, Patricia Jane Moore, etc.

If the bride is the adopted daughter of an unmarried woman:

Miss Nancy Louise Pepper announces the engagement (or marriage) of her adopted daughter, Patricia Jane Moore, to, etc.

WEARING THE ENGAGEMENT RING

The engagement ring is not worn in public until after the engagement has been officially announced. The ring may be worn at the engagement announcement party.

BROKEN ENGAGEMENT

If an engagement has been permanently broken, the engagement ring is returned unless the stone originally belonged to the bride's family.

If the engagement is permanently broken, all wedding presents are returned.

If an engagement is permanently broken but invitations to the ceremony have not been sent out, friends may merely be told that the wedding will not take place. See page 59 for the situation where ceremony invitations have been mailed.

A notice of a broken engagement may be sent to the newspaper, but more often it is not. The form is:

Mr. and Mrs. Howard Delman, 19 Palm Drive, announce that the engagement of their daughter, Dorothy, to Mr. Albert Farmer has been broken by mutual consent.

ANNULMENT

A notice of an annulment is not sent to the newspaper.

An annulment restores a woman's maiden name and the right to again use "Miss."

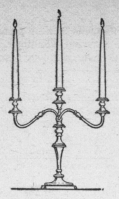

Chapter 2. Types of Weddings

The formality of any wedding depends entirely upon the type of wedding dress the bride wears, not upon the time of day the wedding is held.

ULTRA-FORMAL

The ultra-formal wedding is almost without exception held in a church. When the parents of the bride live in a spacious home and can command the assistance of decorators, florists, skilled domestic help, and a staff of professional wedding consultants and secretaries, a setting suitable for the occasion may be achieved at home or in the garden.

If the wedding takes place in a church, every minute detail of the decorating is supervised by artistic florists and decorators. Music fills the air as the church organist plays the mighty organ, sometimes joined by a chorus of voices.

The bride is her loveliest in a regal gown, either an heirloom or one designed by a famous designer, with full cathedral train and flowing veil.

There are from six to twelve bridal attendants and many more ushers. The church is crowded with ladies in beautiful gowns and men in formal attire. The reception is in the form of a dinner, either seated or semi-buffet. The food is abundant and skillfully prepared by proficient chefs. The wines are superb and plentiful.

Everything is perfection done by perfectionists.

The ultra-formal or formal wedding may be military with full military regalia. The ceremony may be a single or a double ring service.

If the marriage takes place in the church, it must be the first marriage for the bride. Church rules govern whether or not a divorced groom may be married in the church.

In the East the ultra-formal or formal wedding is scheduled at noon, or four or four-thirty in the afternoon. In the South, Midwest, and West it usually takes place in the evening or late afternoon. Formal Catholic weddings take place with Mass before noon.

Engraved invitations, announcements, and enclosure cards are always sent for the formal or ultra-formal wedding.

Clothes are outlined in Chapter 18, "Dress For Weddings."

See also Chapter 22, "The Reception."

FORMAL

The formal wedding takes little less planning than the ultra-formal and the assistance of professionals is needed, although many of the details may be supervised by the mother of the bride.

The formal wedding usually takes place in a church, but it may be held in the home, in the garden, at a private club or suitable ballroom in a hotel.

In the East formal weddings take place at noon, or at four or four-thirty in the afternoon. In the South, Midwest, and West the customary time is evening or late afternoon. Formal Catholic weddings take place with Mass before noon.

There may be from six to twelve bridal attendants, the best man, as many ushers as there are bridesmaids, and as many more ushers as are needed (usually one for every fifty guests invited) to take care of the seating of the guests.

There are always reserved sections for the parents, relatives, and honored guests. If the wedding takes place in the church, there are aisle ribbons, an aisle carpet, pew ribbons, and sometimes a canopy extending from the curb to the church door.

Clothes are outlined in Chapter 18, "Dress For Weddings."

The ceremony may be a single or a double ring service.

The formal wedding is always a first marriage for the

bride. Church rules govern whether or not a divorced groom may be married in the church.

Engraved invitations, announcements, and enclosure cards are always issued for the formal wedding and reception. The handling of these can be done by a bridal secretary, but also can be ably executed by the mother of the bride with the assistance of a bridal counselor.

The formal ceremony is followed by a beautiful reception either in the home or in the garden, or at a private club or hotel where the decorations and food are in keeping with this type of wedding. The food and liquid refreshments are prepared and served by experts, although here again the mother of the bride may take a very active part in planning the menu and other details. There may be a bridal table at the formal reception even though the guests are served buffet style.

There is always music, and dancing very often follows the repast.

With the willing assistance of friends combined with the know-how of professionals, the bride's mother can take a very active part in the planning of her daughter's formal wedding. See Chapter 22, "The Reception."

THE DINNER JACKET

EVENING ONLY—AFTER SIX

There has probably been more discussion about the wearing of the dinner jacket at weddings, especially for wedding attire in the evening, than about any other article of men's clothing. Properly, the dinner jacket is not formal dress for evening, but it is worn as such, particularly by the younger men. Dinner jackets are not worn as a substitute for ultra-formal or formal dress; but with the trend toward casual living, they are worn in some locations even when the bride wears a long length bridal grown and the wedding has a formal feeling.

Location plays a large part in determining whether or not the dinner jacket is the correct attire for an evening wedding. In the casual South and in the Far West the dinner jacket is seen at every sort of evening function. If there is any doubt as to its correctness, the best solution is to consult a leading haberdashery shop before going ahead with wedding plans.

The dinner jacket is never worn before six in the evening no matter what the location is, but it might be worn en route to a six o'clock wedding where the festivities will run later into the evening.

Consult Chapter 18, "Dress for Weddings," for more information.

Engraved invitations are issued for the dinner jacket formal unless the wedding is very small and friends are invited by handwritten notes.

This wedding has a more-or-less formal feeling. Because of this, the following are about the same as for the formal wedding: the place where it is held; decorations and preparations for the ceremony; the number of attendants; clothes worn by the bride, the bridal attendants, and the mothers; the preparation and serving of food and liquid refreshment; and the decorations at the place of the reception. See Chapter 22, "The Reception."

SEMI-FORMAL

The semi-formal wedding may be held in the church or chapel, in the home or in the garden, at a hotel or a club. Evening and any time in the afternoon is considered proper, except for the semi-formal Catholic wedding, which is customarily held in the morning.

No aisle ribbons, canopy, pew ribbons, or aisle carpet are ordinarily used at the semi-formal wedding.

An organist plays if the ceremony is in the church. If the ceremony is in the home or in the garden, at a club or hotel, arrangements may be made for music for the processional if it is desired.

There are usually two or three attendants to the bride (more if it's a garden wedding), and the groom has his best man and as many ushers as there are bridesmaids plus as many more as are needed to take care of the seating of the guests (one for every fifty guests invited) if the ceremony is in church. The semi-formal wedding is usually smaller than the formal wedding, although it need not be. It may be followed by a small or large reception.

Clothes are outlined in Chapter 18, "Dress for Weddings."

The ceremony may be a double or a single ring service.

Church rules govern whether or not a divorced bride or groom may be married in the church.

If the wedding is small, friends are usually invited by word of mouth or by handwritten notes. If the wedding is large, engraved invitations are ordinarily sent. Engraved announcements are often sent after the semi-formal wedding.

Decorations are usually simple, at both the place of the ceremony and that of the reception. Many times the decorations are done by friends or members of the family.

If the home reception is large, food and liquid refreshment are often prepared and served by a caterer and his staff. The small home reception is often prepared by the bride's mother, with the assistance of friends and relatives.

There may be music at the reception, but dancing does not usually follow. See Chapter 22, "The Reception."

INFORMAL

The informal wedding may be held in a church or chapel, in the home or garden, at a club or hotel, at the rectory, or before a magistrate.

The informal wedding may be held at any time during the morning or afternoon. It is not usually scheduled in the evening although it may be. Catholic weddings without the Mass often take place in the afternoon, but they are not held after sundown. Jewish marriages are not performed on a Sabbath. During Lent, Holy Week, and certain holy days, Catholic marriages are not allowed to take place.

Engraved invitations are unnecessary for the informal wedding. Guests are invited verbally or by handwritten notes. The bride's mother or a relative issues the invitations, unless the bride is an orphan or is living where there are no relatives available, in which case a friend may issue the invitations. See "Telephoned Invitations," p. 61.

Correct dress is listed in Chapter 18, "Dress for Weddings."

There are no formal attendants, but the two legal witnesses who are needed to sign the marriage certificate are considered to be the maid (or matron) of honor and the best man.

Decorations are optional. If used, they are very simple. A few flowers and greenery are all that are necessary. Since there is no processional, music is not used. When a reception follows, a friend may be asked to play the piano or a phonograph may be used.

All guests arrive at the designated place a few minutes before the ceremony starts. Guests are greeted by the bride's mother, or father if her mother is deceased. There is no formal seating of guests.

Just before the ceremony starts, the minister takes his place and is followed by the groom and the best man, who usually enter from a side door. The groom's parents take their places in front of the minister, leaving room for the bride and her parents. The bride's mother then goes forward and stands in a position reserved for her. Other guests stand wherever space is available. The maid (or matron) of honor takes her place. The bride enters on her father's arm and the ceremony proceeds.

After the ceremony the groom kisses the bride and, turning around, receives the congratulations of their guests.

A reception may or may not be held afterwards, but at the home wedding a reception of some sort customarily follows the ceremony. This may be held in the same room or in an adjoining one. Wedding cake and punch are the usual refreshments served but the menu may vary according to taste and to the time of day. All guests are expected to remain for the reception if it is held at the same location as the ceremony.

If the reception is held at another location, the guest list may be limited to members of the immediate family, close friends, and attendants, or additional guests may be invited.

When the bride and groom are being entertained after the ceremony at a restaurant, the hostess may find it advisable to contact the head waiter in advance to select the food to be served. If the group is quite small, guests may choose from the regular restaurant menu. A restaurant should be notified as to the plans, and the management is usually happy to supply wedding cake, flowers, and any necessary additional service. If a reception is being held at a public restaurant, a private dining room should be reserved because the gaiety of the party may disturb other guests.

If a seated meal follows the ceremony, place cards may be used or the guests may seat themselves informally, the bride sitting on the right of the groom. See Chapter 22, "The Reception."

This procedure for an informal wedding is equally correct in a home, a hotel, or a chapel.

If the chapel is used and refreshments are desired, arrangements can be made for them to be served in the church parlor. If this is not desired, the bride and groom leave the chapel after having received the best wishes of their friends.

This procedure also pertains to the informal wedding held in a hotel, except that the hotel dining room facilities could be made available for any desired refreshments.

Announcements may be sent after the informal wedding. See Chapter 7, "Announcements."

WEDDINGS AT HOME

For invitations see "Home Weddings," p. 52.

ATTENDANTS

For the formal home wedding the bride usually has no more than four bridesmaids (more if the wedding is in the garden) and sometimes a flower girl.

For the semi-formal home wedding there are usually two attendants, the maid or matron of honor for the bride and the best man for the groom. Sometimes a flower girl is also used.

For the informal home wedding there are no formal attendants, but two legal witnesses are necessary to sign the marriage certificate and are considered to be the maid (or matron) of honor and the best man.

WHAT TO WEAR?

See Chapter 18, "Dress for Weddings." Clothes are the same as for a church wedding of the same formality held at the same time of the day or evening.

THE INFORMAL RECTORY OR PARSONAGE WEDDING

As a general rule the rectory or parsonage is quite small so very few guests are invited to the ceremony. Usually the parents of the bride and the groom and two legal witnesses are all who are present. If space permits and the minister is agreeable, more friends may be invited. Many times members of the minister's household or staff act as witnesses and there are no invited guests or attendants present. Jewish weddings often take place in the rabbi's study.

If invitations are issued they are either telephoned or hand-written to each guest.

The minister is contacted ahead of time to schedule a definite date and time for the ceremony.

If a reception is held afterwards, the bride may wear a wedding gown, but more often there is no reception and she would choose to wear a suit or dress with a hat and gloves. A small corsage given to her by the groom could complete her costume. The bride removes her gloves before the ceremony starts.

The groom wears a business suit or the attire listed on page 185.

Decorations are not used and there is no music.

The groom pays the minister's fee before the ceremony starts.

When all are assembled, the minister takes his place, the bride and the groom stand before him (the bride on the groom's left), and the service is read.

If the bride's father or some other relative is not present, the "giving away" part of the ceremony is done by the bride herself. After the ceremony those present congratulate the bride and groom.

After the rectory wedding there may be a reception either at the bride's home, at the home of a witness, or in a private dining room at a hotel, club, or restaurant. Breakfast, luncheon, or dinner may be served, either seated or buffet-style. Light refreshments are often served, especially if the reception is held at about tea time or after dinner.

If there is a reception after the rectory wedding, all guests invited to the ceremony are invited to the reception and as many more friends as the couple wishes. If the reception is held at a restaurant, guests may choose from the regular menu or the hostess, by contacting the head waiter a few days before the reception, may arrange a special menu. If the reception is seated, place cards may be used or guests may seat themselves informally, the bride sitting at the right of the groom.

There may be a wedding cake and wine is often served.

There is no receiving line at the reception. The bride and groom stand side by side and receive the good wishes of their friends.

Announcements may be sent after the rectory or parsonage wedding. See Chapter 7, "Announcements."

CIVIL CEREMONIES

Civil ceremonies are performed in the judge's chambers by a judge or in the registrar's office by the registrar. They may also be held at home, at the home of a friend, or at a hotel or club, and may be performed by a judge, a justice of the peace, the Mayor, the Governor, or certain other officials of the state or nation. See Catholic civil marriage, p. 219, and Jewish civil marriage, p. 213.

Two legal witnesses are necessary. Guests may be invited, the number depending upon the size of the place of the ceremony. If space is limited, a few friends may be invited to the ceremony and a larger number to any festivities afterwards.

Invitations are issued by word of mouth, by telephone, or by handwritten notes. If there is a reception afterwards, all guests invited to the ceremony are invited to the reception and as many more friends as the couple wishes.

All members of the wedding party arrive at the place of the ceremony before the scheduled time.

The bride wears a street-length dress or suit and wears a corsage instead of carrying a bouquet. Hat and gloves are worn if the place of the ceremony calls for them. The bride removes her gloves before the ceremony starts.

The groom wears a business suit, not slacks with a sport shirt.

The bride and groom go to the registrar's office, where they are met by members of the families and invited guests. When none of these is present, members of the registrar's office staff act as witnesses.

When all are assembled, the bride and groom stand before the registrar and he reads the service.

Unless some designated relative or sponsor is present, the "giving away" part of the ceremony is done by the bride herself or is frequently omitted.

After the ceremony those present congratulate the groom and wish the bride happiness.

Receptions, although perfectly correct, are rarely held after the civil ceremony.

If a justice of the peace or the registrar performs the ceremony, his fee is a set amount (from ten to twenty-five dollars). The fee, enclosed in a white envelope, is given to him by the groom before the ceremony. If a high-ranking official who is a friend of the family performs the ceremony, no fee is expected. A thank-you note should be written to him afterwards and a small gift is appropriate. He is also invited to any festivities after the ceremony.

Announcements may be sent after the civil marriage. See "Announcements," Chapter 7, p. 75.

Also see informal wedding, p. 12.

THE MINISTER'S WEDDING

A minister is married in his bride's church by the bride's minister. If her church is also his church, he is married there by some other minister of their faith. The bride's parents issue the invitations and pay the usual expenses of the ceremony and of the reception. Preparations for the minister's wedding are the same as for any other wedding of the same degree of formality.

If a minister is being married in the church where he officiates, invitations are frequently sent to the entire mailing list of the church. The bride's parents issue the invitations the same as for any other marriage.

In small, less formal communities a minister sometimes invites his entire congregation to the ceremony from the pulpit, making certain it is understood that EVERY member is invited so that no one feels slighted. Any other friends who are not members of his church are invited by word of mouth or by notes written by the bride's mother.

Frequently when a bride has traveled a long way to be married in the church where her groom is the minister, or if the bride has no relatives of her own, the ladies of the church prepare and serve the reception.

A minister who has not yet had his church appointment may be married in a religious ceremony anywhere.

It might be noted here that if a minister performs the marriage service of his daughter, he does not give her away; instead she is escorted down the aisle by some other male member of the family. She is then either given away by the same male member of the family who escorted her or by the bride's mother.

It might also be noted that if a minister's son is being married, the father customarily performs the ceremony, assisted by the minister of the bride's church.

Invitations for the minister's wedding are the same as for any other wedding. See wedding invitations, Chapter 4.

★THE DOUBLE RING CEREMONY

In the double ring ceremony the bride and the groom give each other wedding rings. The best man is in charge of the

ring for the bride. The maid or matron of honor is in charge
of the ring for the groom, which she wears on her finger
until the appropriate time in the ceremony.

The groom wears his ring on the third finger right or left
hand, whichever is preferable.

The groom's ring is a gift from the bride, just as her ring
is a gift from the groom. His ring need not match hers
although it usually does.

DOUBLE WEDDINGS

Invitations and announcement forms for double weddings
are explained in Chapters 7, p. 80 and 4, p. 51.

In the double wedding the brides may use the same attendants or they may each have their own. In any case they
each have their own maid (or matron) of honor. Frequently
the brides act as maid of honor for each other and each
groom may attend the other as best man.

ALTERNATE PROCEDURES

1. . . .

Ushers walk in pairs, one from each group of attendants,
and take their places at different sides of the altar.

Bridesmaids follow, one from each group of attendants,
and take their places at different sides of the altar.

Honor attendants next walking together take their places at
different sides of the altar.

Brides follow, the elder bride and her father first. If the
brides are sisters, both brides may be escorted by the father,
one on each arm; or the elder sister enters first, escorted by
her father, and the younger sister follows, escorted by a male
relative.

2. . . .

Ushers walk in pairs, one from each group of attendants,
and take their places at different sides of the altar.

Bridesmaids of the elder bride follow.

Honor attendant of the elder bride comes next.

The elder bride and her father follow.

Bridesmaids of the younger bride then proceed.

Honor attendant of the younger bride comes next.

The younger bride and her father follow. If the brides are
sisters, the younger bride may be escorted by a male relative;

or the father may escort the elder bride and return to the back of the church to escort the younger bride.

Whichever procedure is used, the elder bride goes down the aisle first and her marriage ceremony is performed first.

If the church has two main aisles, each bridal party may enter and leave by its own aisle.

The processional and recessional positions and the positions at the altar are much more complicated for the double wedding and are best worked out by the minister. Plenty of time should be set aside for the wedding rehearsal and every member must be present.

Mothers of the brides may sit together in the church, leaving room for the fathers, or the younger bride's mother may sit in the second pew. Seating arrangements must be worked out by the families together with the assistance of the minister.

Attention is called to the variation in the formation of the receiving line at the double wedding. See receiving line, p. 237.

MILITARY WEDDING

A military wedding carries with it certain traditions that demand rigid adherence. A girl who is marrying a member of the armed forces must inform herself regarding the etiquette and thus be prepared to cope with it. Certain officers are always sent invitations, some of whom are assigned special seats of honor at the church and at the reception. If the bride-to-be is not an army or navy daughter, she would be wise to consult an experienced wife or mother on her fiance's post before going ahead with any plans for her wedding. See page 42.

See Chapter 12, "Addressing Invitations and Announcements," p. 108, for invitations to be sent to military personnel.

For ceremony and reception invitations for women of the armed forces, see page 90 for military wedding.

WHO MAY HAVE A MILITARY WEDDING?

A military wedding may be held when the groom is a commissioned officer in the regular Navy, Army, Marine Corps, Air Force, or Coast Guard, or if he is a reserve officer on active duty with any of the above forces. Enlisted men in the Navy may also have a formal military ceremony using rifles (instead of swords) for the arch.

TYPE OF WEDDING

Military weddings are usually ultra-formal or formal church weddings. A military wedding can be semi-formal, but it is never informal.

WHERE IS IT HELD?

Most military weddings are held in the church although occasionally one is held in the home or garden.

MINISTER OR CHAPLAIN?

If the bride's father is an active member of the armed forces, the chaplain of the father's post should perform the marriage ceremony.

If the bride and her father are civilians, she may have the minister of her choice, either her own minister or her fiance's chaplain.

Service chaplains do not accept a fee for the performance of the marriage ceremony.

BOUTONNIERES

No boutonnieres or flowers are worn with a military uniform.

MEDALS AND RIBBONS

With the regulation uniform, medal ribbons are worn.
With the dress uniform, large medals are worn.
With the mess or dinner jacket, miniature medals are worn.

ATTENDANTS

The groom's attendants are fellow officers. There are occasions when some of his attendants are civilian; and if this is the case, the civilian ushers are paired together in the processional and recessional, as are the officers. Many times the best man is civilian.

Civilian ushers take no part in the arch of sabers or swords.

The groom has as many ushers as there are bridesmaids and/or as many as are needed for the seating of the guests (usually one for every fifty guests invited).

The bride's attendants are the same friends who would attend her at a civilian wedding, the number depending upon the formality and location of the wedding, the same as for any other wedding.

THE ARCH OF SWORDS OR SABERS

Only officers may take part in the arch of swords or sabers.

If the arch takes place outside the church (and it usually does as most churches will not permit the drawing of swords inside the church), the ushers precede the bride and groom in the recessional, or they may leave by a side door in order to be ready at the front door when the bride and groom arrive there. As the bride and groom arrive at the front entrance, the head usher gives the command "Draw swords" (Navy) or "Draw sabers" (Army), and the bride and groom pass under the arch. No one else passes under the arch. The remaining attendants wait inside the church until after the head usher gives the command "Return swords" or "Return sabers."

If the arch of swords or sabers takes place inside the church, the officers step forward as the bride and groom start down the aisle in the recessional, and, at the head usher's command, they draw swords or sabers. After the bride and groom have passed under the arch, the command is given "Return swords (or sabers)" and the remaining members of the bridal party leave in the usual manner. Only the bride and the groom pass under the arch.

The arch of swords or sabers may be used whether the wedding takes place in a church or elsewhere. To permit the guests at the wedding ceremony to witness the arch of swords this procedure may be used:

Following the ceremony at the altar the wedding party leaves in the usual recessional order. The bride, groom, and bridesmaids go immediately to an isolated location in the church or to the vestry or anteroom near the church entrance, there to wait until all the guests are outside. This discourages the usual congratulatory conversation and thus facilitates the clearing of the church. The mothers, relatives, and honored guests are escorted in the usual manner to the church vestibule from where they proceed outside and take a favorable position to observe the arch of swords. Other guests leave the church as quickly as possible. The ushers then take their positions. The bride, groom, and bridesmaids return to the church vestibule and the arch proceeds in the usual manner.

WEARING SWORD OR SABER WHILE USHERING

The military ushers do not wear their swords or sabers while ushering guests. They are put on just before the processional starts.

WHAT TO WEAR?

The way in which the bride dresses determines the degree of formality of the entire wedding.

The bride and her attendants, mothers, relatives, and women guests dress according to the formality of the wedding. See dress chart, Chapter 18.

The groom and his military attendants wear regulation summer or winter dress uniform, the type prescribed by his particular branch of service. If the wedding is less formal or if the officer is not required to own a dress uniform, Army olive-drab or Navy blues may be worn.

Military fathers follow the dress status of the groom. Nonmilitary fathers dress in accordance with civilian custom.

Nonmilitary attendants wear the same attire as they would at a civilian wedding of the same degree of formality and held at the same time of the day or evening.

Military men guests follow the dress status of the groom. Civilian men guests dress in accordance with civilian custom.

If an officer's wedding is semi-formal or informal, he may wear a uniform or (unless regulations forbid) civilian attire, the type listed in Chapter 18, "Dress for Weddings."

WOMEN OF THE SERVICE

Women of the armed forces may wear a uniform or (unless regulations forbid) a wedding dress.

DECORATIONS

Decorations at the church and at the place of the reception may include regimental flags. (Consult the minister before making plans for decorations.)

GROOMSMEN OR USHERS?

The groom's military ushers are sometimes called groomsmen.

RECEPTION

Cutting the wedding cake:

The groom's sword or saber is used to cut the first slice of wedding cake, from the bottom tier. The groom places his right hand over the right hand of the bride as they cut together. They then share the slice of cake.

BEST MAN'S TOAST

The best man proposes the first toast at the reception, and it usually welcomes the bride into the service as well as wishing the couple happiness. Other toasts follow. See Chapter 22, "The Reception."

INTRODUCTIONS

An officer's rank must be recognized and used in introductions.

ENLISTED MEN

The arch of swords or sabers is never used at an enlisted man's wedding. A Navy enlisted man may use an arch of rifles. An enlisted man may be married in uniform and attended by other men in uniform or (unless regulations forbid) may wear civilian clothes. See dress chart, Chapter 18.

An enlisted man serving at someone else's wedding wears his uniform or (unless regulations forbid) civilian clothes. See dress chart, Chapter 18.

NONMILITARY WEDDINGS FOR OFFICERS

An officer is not compelled to have a military wedding. Many are married in regular church or home ceremonies, either formal, semi-formal, or informal. He and his attendants may wear a uniform or (unless regulations forbid) the same attire as for a civilian wedding of the same degree of formality.

The Second Marriage

THE YOUNG WIDOW

Some churches do not allow a second marriage to be held in the church. If it is allowed, however, there is no reason why the young widow should not be married there.

A small second marriage does not require engraved invitations; guests are usually invited verbally or by handwritten notes. If the wedding is large, engraved invitations may be sent. See pages 55-56. Engraved announcements are often sent. See Chapter 7, "Announcements."

The young widow may have one or two attendants; and if she has a small daughter of suitable age, she may attend her mother, also.

A second marriage is usually informal with a restricted number of guests, existing conditions governing this somewhat. A larger number of guests may be invited to the reception following the ceremony.

The groom usually has one attendant and the best man, or only the best man if the bride has but one attendant.

The young widow's father may escort her down the aisle and give her away, or she need not be given away.

The young widow does not wear all white, a flowing veil, a train, or a formal wedding gown.

THE MORE MATURE WIDOW

The more mature widow will probably choose an informal church or chapel wedding (church rules permitting), a home wedding, or a civil ceremony.

The mature widow issues her own informal invitations, either by handwritten notes or verbally. If engraved invitations are sent, they are usually issued by the bride and groom themselves, although they may be issued by a member of the bride's family. See page 56.

The mature widow has one attendant; if she has a daughter of suitable age, she may be her mother's attendant. The groom also has one attendant.

The mature widow is not given away nor does she walk down the aisle.

The mature widow does not wear all white, a flowing veil, a train, or formal wedding dress.

The mature widow may give her own reception.

THE YOUNG DIVORCEE

The divorcee's marriage is seldom held in a church. The divorced woman usually chooses a civil ceremony, and she and her groom have one attendant each. Any daughters by a former marriage do not attend their mother.

A divorcee's marriage is usually simple, with a restricted number of guests, although it may be followed by a larger reception.

The bride need not be given away.

Invitations are issued by handwritten notes or verbally. Engraved invitations are very seldom sent for the divorcee's marriage. Engraved announcements may be sent. See p. 79.

A bride who has been married before does not wear all white, a formal wedding gown, a long flowing veil, or a train. Her headdress is usually a small hat with a short veil, and her flowers are a corsage instead of a bridal bouquet.

Gifts should not be expected for a second marriage, although many friends will send them.

THE OLDER DIVORCEE

The same rules apply as for the young divorcee. The older divorcee never sends engraved invitations. Engraved announcements may be sent. See page 79.

Secret Marriages

Engraved announcements may be issued by the bride's parents after the secret marriage or elopement. An announcement of the marriage may be sent to the newspaper. The exact date, year, and place the marriage took place must be included in both announcements. See p. 80 for engraved announcement form.

If engraved announcements are not sent, the bride's mother may write informal notes to friends informing them of the marriage. The older bride and groom often issue their own engraved announcements, or the bride may write notes to inform friends.

Even if the marriage has been kept secret for many weeks, engraved announcements may still be sent by the bride's parents, stating the exact date, year, and place the ceremony took place; or the bride's mother may write informal notes informing friends and relatives of the marriage.

The Mature Bride's First Marriage

The mature bride may have a formal church wedding, but more often she does not. Simplicity and sophistication are the keynotes of the older bride's wedding; and she usually chooses a small informal home, church, chapel, or civil ceremony. She may or may not be given away by her father or some other male member of her family, or by a close friend.

She may walk down the aisle; but more often she waits in the vestry with the groom, best man, and the matron (or maid) of honor until the ceremony is ready to start. When the minister is ready to start, the bride, groom, best man, and the matron of honor take their places at the chancel.

Engraved invitations may be issued by the bride's parents but are more often issued by the bride and groom themselves. Guests may be invited by handwritten notes or verbally by the bride. See page 57.

The more mature bride may wear white or a formal wedding dress with veil and carry a bridal bouquet; but most mature brides prefer to be married in a more informal style, wearing a dressy suit or gown with a small hat and a corsage. If a formal wedding is planned, one or two attendants for the bride and one or two for the groom are the rule. If the ceremony is informal, two legal witnesses are all that are necessary.

A small informal home, church, chapel, or civil ceremony may be followed by a larger reception. The mature bride may give her own reception, or it may be given at the home of friends or relatives. See Chapter 22, "The Reception."

Announcements may be issued by the bride's parents or by the bride and the groom. See page 78.

The Groom's Second Marriage

The fact that the groom has been married before may prevent the couple from marrying in certain churches; otherwise, it has no effect whatsoever upon the wedding plans of the bride. If this is HER first marriage, she may wear a formal gown and veil and have as many attendants as she would if this were the groom's first marriage.

The Wedding Hour and Date

The DATE of any wedding must be approved by the officiating minister (rabbi, priest).

Jewish weddings are not held on their Sabbath (Friday evening at sundown until Saturday evening at sundown) and they are not held on High Holydays. The rabbi must be consulted before deciding upon a wedding date.

Catholic weddings are not held after sundown, during Lent and Holy Week, and on certain holy days. The priest must be consulted before a wedding date can be scheduled.

FORMAL PROTESTANT

Four, four-thirty, or five in the afternoon; at high noon; in some locations in the evening, six or after.

FORMAL CATHOLIC

Before noon with the High Mass.

FORMAL JEWISH

The same as formal Protestant.

SEMI-FORMAL PROTESTANT AND JEWISH

The same as formal; also a semi-formal wedding may be scheduled at any time in the afternoon.

SEMI-FORMAL CATHOLIC

Early in the morning with the Low Mass.

INFORMAL PROTESTANT AND JEWISH

Any time during the morning or afternoon. Informal weddings are very seldom scheduled in the evening, although they may be.

INFORMAL CATHOLIC

Catholic weddings without the Mass often take place in the afternoon, five o'clock being the favorite hour.

Chapter 3. Consulting the Minister

The terms "church" and "minister" are used for simplification and should be mentally translated into the proper terminology for a particular religion, i.e., "church" to take the meaning of Synagogue or Temple and "minister" to designate priest or rabbi.

After the engagement has been announced and the bride and groom have decided upon a tentative date, the time, and the type of wedding it is to be, no more plans can be made until the minister is consulted and his approval granted.

THE BRIDE AND HER MOTHER VISIT THE MINISTER

If the wedding is to be in the church or if a minister is performing the ceremony somewhere else and the bride's mother is handling the details of the wedding, the bride and her mother must make a visit to the minister in order to see if the date and time selected meet with his approval and if it will fit into the church schedule. Invitations cannot be ordered nor can any other plans be made for the wedding until after he has approved all plans.

MAKE AN APPOINTMENT

An appointment with the minister should be made through the church secretary. Plenty of time should be set aside for this visit as there are many questions to ask. The appointment should be kept promptly. The same kind of clothes are worn as would be worn to church.

28

SETTING THE DATE AND TIME OF THE CEREMONY

The date and time selected must fit into the church schedule and both are subject to the minister's approval. There are certain days and hours a wedding may not be scheduled.

REHEARSAL DATE AND TIME

The date and time of the rehearsal must fit into the church schedule and it should be decided upon at this visit.

A VISITING MINISTER

Often it is desired to have a visiting minister perform the ceremony. If this is the case, the regular minister must give his consent. It is allowed in some churches and not allowed in others.

If the visiting minister performs the ceremony, both he and the regular minister are given a fee by the groom, unless the former is such a close friend or relative that no fee should be offered.

If the visiting minister performs the ceremony and he comes from out of town, his traveling expenses and hotel bills are paid by the family to whom he is rendering this kindness.

FEES FOR THE CHURCH STAFF

The minister may be asked what is the usual fee for any church staff member who assists at the ceremony, such as organist, sexton, candle-lighters.

RULES OF DRESS

The rules of dress for both participants and guests should be discussed; there may be some rules regarding sleeveless dresses, head-covering, etc.

SEATING CAPACITY

If the ceremony is to include a large number of guests, it is wise to ask about the seating capacity of the church in order to avoid inviting more guests than the church will seat comfortably.

MILITARY WEDDING

There are many specific church rules governing a military wedding. If it is to be a military wedding, the minister will have to know this at this time. These rules must be understood before making any further plans.

CHURCH DECORATIONS

Church decorations vary with denominations. Some churches have very strict regulations governing the kind and amount of decoration allowable. Some churches have their own ladies of the church or altar guilds who perform this service. It is best to discuss the decorations at this visit.

PICTURES

Taking pictures is allowed in some churches; in others it is not.

RECORDING OF THE CEREMONY

Recordings can be made of the wedding ceremony, but permission must be obtained from the minister before making arrangements for this.

THE WEDDING MUSIC

The music is discussed at this time. A list of allowable selections may be obtained from the church organist. All selections used by the organist, choir, and soloist must be approved by the minister.

NOTIFYING THE CHURCH STAFF

Any regular members of the church staff, such as organist, soloist, sexton, are usually notified by the church secretary as to the correct time and date of both the ceremony and the rehearsal. It is important that all members of the church staff taking part in the ceremony be notified. It should be made certain that this will be taken care of by the church secretary.

KNEELING CUSHION

When a kneeling cushion is to be used, the church usually supplies it. If a cushion is desired and the church does not have one, the florist or a bridal service will supply it.

CANDLES AND CANDLE HOLDERS

Most churches have an ample supply of candle holders. If, however, the church does not have as many as are needed, the florist can supply more. The minister must approve the use of more than the usual number of candles and the use of candles for aisle decorations. As most churches use special candles, a supply is kept on hand and they are purchased from the church.

CANOPY

Some churches permit the use of an outside canopy and others do not. If one is to be used and the church does not have one, the minister will know where one can be rented.

AISLE CARPET, AISLE DECORATIONS, AISLE RIBBONS

The aisle decorations must be discussed.

The aisle carpet (or canvas) and the aisle ribbons are supplied by the florist.

EARLY COMMUNION

Many churches have early communion for the bride and groom and members of the immediate families the day of the ceremony; the minister will advise as to this.

THE BRIDE AND GROOM VISIT THE MINISTER

The church secretary should be called and an appointment made with the minister. There are many questions to ask the minister and many that the minister will want to ask, so plenty of time should be allowed for this visit. This appointment should be kept promptly. The same dress is worn as would be worn to church.

HE DECIDES THE DATE AND THE TIME

Although a tentative date and time for the wedding have been selected, the minister must give his approval. There are certain days and times that a wedding may not be scheduled; the date and time of the ceremony and the rehearsal must fit into the church schedule.

BAPTISM AND CONFIRMATION CERTIFICATES

When the appointment is made, the church secretary is asked if any papers are required, such as baptism or confirmation certificates. If called for these papers are taken on this visit. These documents might be required especially if the groom is a stranger to the minister or if he is of a different denomination.

OF ANOTHER FAITH

If either the bride or the groom is of another faith, the minister may require some religious instruction for that party. If either the bride or the groom is of a different faith and is considering joining the church of the other, this too must be discussed.

THE WEDDING SERVICE PROCEDURE

Procedure for the processional and the recessional and the positions of the participants at the altar are all decided by the minister, and his decision should not be questioned. He is the only one who knows how the wedding service should be conducted in his church.

THE MINISTER'S FEE

It is perfectly proper to ask the minister or the church secretary the usual amount paid the minister for his services.

CHURCH RULES

Any specific religious rules pertaining to the ceremony will be explained at this visit and any that are not understood may be asked about at this time. The minister will be happy to explain them.

DOUBLE RING

If the ceremony is to be double ring, the minister will want to know this at this visit.

MUSIC

A favorite or special musical selection, not listed on the approved list, must be sanctioned by the minister before it can be used.

EARLY COMMUNION

Many churches have early communion for the bride and groom and members of the immediate families on the day of the ceremony. The minister will advise here.

ORDER OF THE RECESSION

Permission must be obtained from the minister before plans are made to have the ushers and the bridesmaids leave the church in couples.

Chapter 4. Information on Reception, Ceremony, and Announcement Forms

WHERE TO ORDER

Invitations, announcements, and enclosure cards may be ordered at most fine jewelers, the engravers, a bridal consultant shop, the printers, many gift shops, some department stores, and specialty shops.

WHEN TO ORDER

After the date, time, place, and type of wedding have been decided upon; the minister has been consulted about the date, time, and type; and the place of the reception has been engaged; the invitations, announcements, and enclosure cards may be ordered.

Engraved invitations should be ordered at least two months before the date of the ceremony, as they take some time to prepare.

Printed invitations take less time than engraved ones and may be ordered six to seven weeks before the ceremony.

Enclosure cards and announcements are ordered at the same time as the invitations.

Stationery to be used for handwritten invitations or personal notes may be ordered or purchased at the stationery store or department store. If it is to be engraved, it should be ordered seven to eight weeks before the ceremony.

How Many to Order

Of course the number of invitations to order will depend upon the size of the wedding and the reception, but it is best to order a few more than the number of invited guests as there may be mistakes in addressing.

If engraved invitations are being used and it is found that the original order is insufficient, more can be ordered and delivered in a few days, as the original plate is kept on file until after the wedding date. After the wedding the original plate is sent to the bride and groom in the form of a card or ash tray, so that they will have a permanent memento of the invitation.

If printed invitations are being used, it is best to order many more than is thought necessary. This is much cheaper than placing another order.

Engraved Invitations

Nothing but an engraved invitation or announcement is correct for the formal wedding. It is better to invite friends by handwritten notes or by telephone than it is to use printed invitations.

Of the many kinds of lettering used for engraved invitations the most popular and the least expensive is the well-known script. There are a number of styles from which to select; all are pretty and in good taste.

Process Printed Invitations

Printed invitations or announcements are never used for a formal wedding and should never be used for any wedding held in a church, no matter how small.

Printed invitations or announcements are sometimes used to economize, although this is a very poor place to do so. If they are used they must not deviate from the engraved form.

There is a raised printed invitation made by process lettering that is less expensive than engraved invitations but looks very similar. If printed invitations are being considered in order to economize, process or raised lettering is the accepted choice.

Paper

Select the highest quality paper; the difference in the price is very little.

SIZE

Conventional invitations are the folded type with the engraving on the front page. There is, however, a smaller unfolded invitation that can be purchased.

If any enclosure cards are to be included in the invitation, it has been proven that the larger folded type invitation is by far the most practical one to use, as the smaller enclosed card is inserted between the folds of the folded invitation and there is no chance of it being lost or overlooked.

COLOR

Practically all wedding invitations are white or creamy white. They may be obtained in pastels, but white and creamy white are the accepted colors.

"HONOUR OF YOUR PRESENCE"

The expression "honour of your presence" is used on all church ceremony invitations and on the combination church ceremony and reception invitation.

"PLEASURE OF YOUR COMPANY"

The expression "pleasure of your company" is used on all reception invitations and on some ceremony invitations when the ceremony is to be held somewhere other than the church.

R.S.V.P.

R.S.V.P. (*Repondez, s'il vous plait*) means "reply, if you please."

An invitation for the church ceremony carries no R.S.V.P. as it needs no answer.

All invitations to a reception or breakfast after the ceremony include an R.S.V.P.

All home, garden, club, or hotel ceremony invitations include an R.S.V.P., as refreshments are usually served afterwards and arrangements must be made.

"Kindly respond". . ."R.S.V.P.". . ."R.s.v.p.". . ."The favour of a reply is requested". . ."Please reply". . ."The favour of a reply is requested to". . ."Please send reply to". . ."Kindly send response to". . . are all equally correct to use.

If a reply is requested to a home ceremony invitation or

reception invitation and the reply is to be sent to an address other than that included in the body of the invitation, the reply address is added in the lower left hand corner of the invitation. Such as:

Please reply to
56 Allenhurst Street

RECEPTION OR BREAKFAST

"Breakfast" is the word used if it takes place before 1 P.M. "Reception" is the word used if it takes place after 1 P.M.

HOW THE NAMES OF THE BRIDE AND GROOM ARE LINKED

The word "to" is used to link the names of the bride and the groom on the ceremony or the combination ceremony and reception invitation.

The word "and" is used to link the names of the bride and the groom on the reception invitation.

THE WORDS "HONOUR" AND "FAVOUR"

The words "honour" and "favour" are always spelled with a *u*.

THE TIME OF THE CEREMONY

The time of the ceremony is written: "at half after five o'clock". . ."at five o'clock." Quarter hours are not used. Since A.M. and P.M. are never used, the words "in the morning" or "in the evening" may be, particularly when the ceremony is at eight or nine o'clock.

Roman Catholic wedding invitations often show the phrase "Nuptial High Mass" or "Nuptial Mass." Such an invitation might read:

at eleven o'clock Nuptial Mass

DAYLIGHT SAVING TIME

If the ceremony or reception is during daylight saving time, avoid confusion by having it engraved into the invitation:

at five o'clock, daylight saving time

THE CHURCH ADDRESS

If the city is very large and the church is not a landmark, the church address is included in the invitation such as:

First Presbyterian Church
1015 North Boulevard
New Orleans

THE YEAR

The year may be omitted in ceremony and reception invitations, but it *must* be included in the announcement of a marriage. The year line may be correctly written:

One thousand, nine hundred and sixty-five
One thousand nine hundred and sixty-five
one thousand nine hundred and sixty-five

STREET NUMBERS

If a street number is very short, it is written out:

Two Bellaire Circle

If a street number is long, it is written:

7849 Bellaire Circle

CITY AND STATE

The city is always used on wedding invitations and announcements. If the city is very large or one of a kind such as Chicago, Miami, or Baltimore, it is not necessary to mention the state; otherwise the name of the state also appears.

ABBREVIATIONS

If the word "junior" is used, it is written with a small *j*. If it is abbreviated, it is written with a capital *J*: "Jr." If London script is used, it is written "Jun."

The word "Doctor" may be abbreviated "Dr." but more correctly it is written "Doctor." "Doctor" may be abbreviated to "Dr." when "junior" is abbreviated to "Jr."

The word "Saint" is never abbreviated "St." The proper form is:

Saint John's Church

The word "on" may be included or omitted. Such as:

on Friday, the tenth of June

NICKNAMES

Nicknames are *never* used.

INITIALS

Initials are not used on invitations unless the initial is the given name.

WRITING ON THE INVITATION

A message is never handwritten on an engraved invitation.

WHEN DOCTORS' TITLES ARE USED

If the groom and/or the father of the bride are physicians, their titles appear upon the invitations.

If the bride is a physician and her parents issue the invitations or announcements, the bride's title of Doctor is not used. If the bride is a physician and someone other than the bride's parents issue the invitations or announcements, or if she issues them herself in conjunction with the groom, her title of Doctor is used.

If the bride's mother is a physician and she and her husband are issuing the invitations or announcements, she uses Mrs. rather than Doctor. If the bride's mother is a physician and she is issuing the invitations alone, she may use her title of Doctor. She is then Doctor Anna Florence Wright.

Holders of academic doctorates such as Ph.D. may use their title as doctor on invitations or announcements, although they seldom do so unless the holder occupies a very important office such as president of a university; whereas it would appear in bad taste for holders of honorary degrees to use their titles on engraved invitations or announcements.

OTHER TITLES THAT ARE USED

If the groom and/or father of the bride are members of the clergy, their titles appear before their names on the invitations or announcements such as: The Reverend . . . Bishop . . . Rabbi . . . Doctor . . . etc.

Doctors of medicine and dentistry and military and naval officers all use their titles on invitations and announcements.

The letters of degrees are not used on invitations or announcements.

"SECOND" AND "THIRD"

Numerals· II (for second) or III (for third) may be used on invitations or announcements if that person has always been so known.

Roman numerals are separated by a comma:

William Johnson, III

COAT OF ARMS AND FAMILY CREST

A coat of arms or family crest may be embossed (never die-stamped in color) at the top of the invitation or announcement IF the bride's mother AND father are issuing the invitation or announcement, or if it is being issued by some other MALE member of the bride's family.

A coat of arms or family crest is never used when a woman is issuing the invitations alone.

A husband-to-be's coat of arms or family crest is not used on reception or ceremony invitations. A groom's coat of arms or family crest may be used on announcements IF the bride and the groom are issuing their own announcements. A groom's coat of arms or family crest is NOT used on announcements if the bride's family is issuing the announcements.

RETURN ADDRESS

The return address may be embossed, without color, on the flap of the outside envelope of a wedding invitation. A return address is not used upon an announcement. "At home" cards are enclosed with the announcement.

ISSUING THE INVITATIONS

Ceremony invitations are issued by the bride's parents. If one parent is deceased the other, of course, issues the invitations. If both parents are deceased, invitations are issued by a relative, guardian, or a close friend.

There are exceptions to this rule:

1 . . . The wedding of the bride from overseas who has come to this country to be married and has no relative living here may be sponsored by the groom's parents. See the section "Overseas Bride."

2 . . . The young bride, widow, or divorcee who has no relatives may issue her own invitations.

3 ... The mature bride or widow usually issues her own invitations.

WHEN THE GROOM'S FAMILY GIVES THE WEDDING

Circumstances would have to be very unusual for the groom's family to give the wedding, to issue the invitations to their future daughter-in-law's wedding, or to have the wedding at their home. There are, however, unusual circumstances and they would have to be understood by intimate friends before the regular conventions may be disregarded. A bride must not suggest that her wedding be given by the groom's family. This is their prerogative; but if they make the suggestion she may accept if any of the following conditions exist:

1 ... The two families of the bride and the groom are distantly related.

2 ... Both families are very old friends.

3 ... The bride is from overseas and has no relative in this country. See the section, "Overseas Bride."

4 ... The bride's family live so far away that it is impossible for them to attend the wedding.

5 ... The bride's parents are deceased and she has no close friends or relative to sponsor her.

If for some reason the groom's parents do give the wedding and the bride's parents are alive, the invitations are issued in the name of the bride's parents.

The following form may be used for this unusual situation:

Mr. and Mrs. Edward Dawson
request the honour of your presence
at the marriage of
Miss Janice Ann Davenport
to
their son
Henry James Dawson
etc.

INVITATIONS THAT REQUIRE AN ANSWER

An invitation to a church ceremony needs no answer.

All invitations that include a reception or breakfast must be answered.

All home or garden ceremony invitations need an answer

as they generally include some sort of a reception afterwards and arrangements must be made.

All invitations that include an R.S.V.P. must be answered.

CHURCH WEDDING

TRADITIONAL CHURCH CEREMONY FORM

Mr. and Mrs. James Arthur Reid
request the honour of your presence   (take note)
at the marriage of their daughter
Nancy Jane
to
Mr. William Edward Pope
on Friday, the eighth of June   ("on" may be
                                      omitted)
One thousand nine hundred and sixty-five (mention
at five o'clock   of year optional)
Saint John's Church
Ormond, Florida

TRADITIONAL RECEPTION FORMS

If a reception is to follow the ceremony and is to be held some place other than where the ceremony is to take place, the reception time may be scheduled one hour after the ceremony time. If this is done, guests are not kept waiting in a long receiving line while pictures are being made of the wedding party. One reception form is:

Mr. and Mrs. James Arthur Reid
request the pleasure of your company (take note)
Friday the eighth of June
at six o'clock
Grove Hill Club
Ormond, Florida

Kindly respond

Another form:

Mr. and Mrs. James Arthur Reid
request the pleasure of your company (take note)
at the wedding reception   (or breakfast)
following the ceremony
at
Grove Hill Club
Ormond

Please reply

Another form:

> *Reception* (or breakfast)
> *immediately following the ceremony*
> *Grove Hill Club*
> *Ormond*

R.S.V.P.

THE TRADITIONAL COMBINATION CEREMONY AND RECEPTION INVITATION

This form may be used when all guests are invited to the ceremony and the reception, although it would be in much better taste to issue ceremony invitations with a separate reception card enclosed.

> *Doctor and Mrs. James Arthur Reid*
> *request the honour of your presence* (always when
> *at the marriage of their daughter* ceremony is
> *Nancy Jane*   in church)
> *to*   (take note)
> *Mr. William Edward Pope*
> *on Friday, the eighth of June*   ("on" may be
>   omitted)
> *One thousand nine hundred and sixty-five* (mention
> *at five o'clock*   of year optional)
> *Saint John's Church*
> *and afterward at*
> *Grove Hill Club*

Please send reply to
Two Dewitt Drive

If the reception is to be much later than the ceremony, the time also is included, such as:

> *and afterward at*
> *seven o'clock*
> *Grove Hill Club*

R.S.V.P.
Two Dewitt Drive

WRITE-IN INVITATION

Although it is more individual, the write-in invitation is used very little because of the extra amount of work involved. The invitation is engraved with blank spaces in which to write the names of guests, instead of requesting the honour of "your" presence. The form is:

> *Doctor and Mrs. James Arthur Reid*
> *request the honour of*
> *Doctor and Mrs. Walter Pierce Scott's**
> *presence at the marriage of their daughter*
> *Nancy Jane*
> *to*
> *etc.*

With this type of invitation a reception card of the same kind is enclosed. The form is:

> *Doctor and Mrs. James Arthur Reid*
> *request the pleasure of*
> *Doctor and Mrs. Walter Pierce Scott's**
> *company, on Friday, the eighth of June*
> *at half after six o'clock*
> *etc.*

CEREMONY LARGER THAN THE RECEPTION

If fewer guests are invited to the reception than to the ceremony, a reception card is enclosed in the ceremony invitation and sent only to those guests invited to both the reception and the ceremony.

The traditional form ceremony and reception invitations are used.

If the ceremony is to include a large number of guests and only very close friends and relatives are to be invited to the reception or breakfast, the bride's mother may write personal notes inviting these few guests or they may be invited verbally. If the bride's mother writes personal notes inviting these few guests to the reception, the letters or notes are mailed separately; they are NOT enclosed in the ceremony invitation.

CEREMONY SMALLER THAN THE RECEPTION

Here the reception invitation would appear on the larger double sheet; the smaller enclosed card would be the invita-

* Written by hand.

tion to the ceremony and sent to only those few people invited to the ceremony and the reception. The reception invitation form is:

> *Mr. and Mrs. James Arthur Reid*
> *request the pleasure of your company* (take note)
> *at the wedding reception for their daughter*
> *Nancy Jane*
> *and*   ("and" always, on
>   reception invitation)
> *Mr. William Edward Pope, junior*   (or Jr.)
> *Saturday afternoon, the fourth of August*
> *One thousand nine hundred and sixty-five* (year may
> *at half after five o'clock*   be omitted)
> *Richmond Country Club*
> *Richmond, Virginia*

Please respond to
245 Grace Street
(Bride's home address)

If a small engraved ceremony card is enclosed in the reception invitation, it reads:

> *Mr. and Mrs. James Arthur Reid*
> *request the honour of your presence*
> *at the marriage ceremony*
> *at four o'clock*
> *Saint John's Church*

Or:

> *Ceremony at four o'clock*
> *Saint John's Church*

CHURCH CEREMONY—RECEPTION AT FRIEND'S HOME

If the ceremony is to be at the church and the reception at a friend's home, and if the bride's parents are living, the ceremony and the reception invitations are both issued by the bride's parents. For invitations when parents are deceased see Chapter 6, "Deceased Parents."

The traditional ceremony invitation is used, and one of the following forms of reception card is enclosed:

Mr. and Mrs. James Arthur Reid
request the pleasure of your company
Saturday the eighth of December
at half after five o'clock
at the residence of
Mr. and Mrs. Peter Boyd Hays
4560 Country Club Drive
Houston, Texas   (state may be omitted)
Please respond to
200 Habersham

Or:

Reception
following the ceremony   (or immediately
at the residence of   following the
Mr. and Mrs. Peter Boyd Hays ceremony)
4560 Country Club Drive
Houston

Please respond to
200 Habersham
(Bride's home address)

Roman Catholic:

Mr. and Mrs. John Austin Conover
request the honour of your presence
at the Nuptial Mass uniting their daughter
Catherine Mary
    and   (take note)
Mr. Arnold Patrick O'Leary
in the Sacrament of Holy Matrimony
on Saturday, the first of December
One thousand nine hundred and sixty-five
at eleven o'clock
Saint James Roman Catholic Church
Chicago

A reception card may be enclosed with the invitation.

Nuptial Mass

Mr. and Mrs. John Albert O'Connell
request the honour of your presence
at the marriage of their daughter
Mary Elizabeth
to
Mr. Robert Frank Rice
on Thursday, the fourteenth of June
One thousand nine hundred and sixty-five
at eleven o'clock Nuptial Mass
Saint James Catholic Church
Denver

A special enclosure card may be sent to a small group of relatives and intimate friends of the bride and groom and their families, enclosed with the wedding invitation.

You are cordially invited
to join the wedding party
in receiving Holy Communion
at this Nuptial Mass

A reception card may also be enclosed.

Nuptial High Mass

Mr. and Mrs. John Albert O'Connell
request the honour of your presence
at the Nuptial High Mass at which their daughter
Mary Elizabeth
and   (note "and")
Mr. Robert Frank Rice
Will be united in the Sacrament of Holy Matrimony
Thursday the fourteenth of June
One thousand nine hundred and sixty-five
at ten o'clock
Saint James Roman Catholic Church
Denver

A reception card may be enclosed with the invitation.

Hebrew Wedding (at club or hotel)

Mr. and Mrs. Joseph Stanley Wise
request the honour of your presence
at the marriage of their daughter
Barbara Louise
to
Mr. Morris Edward Jacobs
son of
Mr. and Mrs. Edward Morris Jacobs
on Wednesday, the first of August
One thousand nine hundred and sixty-five
at half after three o'clock
Hotel Deauville
Miami Beach, Florida
Reception at five o'clock

Hebrew Wedding (at synagogue)

Mr. and Mrs. Joseph Stanley Wise
Mr. and Mrs. Edward Morris Jacobs
request the honour of your presence
at the marriage of their children   ("children"
Barbara Louise   denotes relationship
and   not age)
Mr. Morris Edward Jacobs
Wednesday the first of August
One thousand nine hundred and sixty-five
at four o'clock
Congregation Ahev Shalom
Seattle

Reception form:

Reception at six o'clock
Arrowhead Country Club

Please reply to
341 Poinsettia Avenue

Wedding Anniversary Invitations

BY THE COUPLE—TO A DINNER AT THEIR HOME

1940   1965
Mr. and Mrs. Oliver James Simpson
request the pleasure of your company
at a dinner to celebrate
the Twenty-Fifth Anniversary of their marriage
on Tuesday, the sixteenth of May
at eight o'clock
4520 Venice Drive
The favour of a reply
is requested

BY THE COUPLE—AT HOME

1940   1965
Mr. and Mrs. Oliver James Simpson
At Home
Tuesday the sixteenth of May
from seven until ten o'clock
4520 Venice Drive

BY THE COUPLE—HOTEL RECEPTION

1940   1965
Mr. and Mrs. Oliver James Simpson
request the pleasure of your company
on their Silver Wedding Anniversary
Tuesday the sixteenth of May
From seven until ten o'clock
Great Room, Carrilon Hotel
Palm Beach

BY THE FAMILY—DINNER AT A CLUB

1940   1965
In honour of
Mr. and Mrs. Oliver James Simpson
their daughters
request the pleasure of your company
at dinner
on Tuesday, the sixteenth of May
at eight o'clock
Country Club of Dayton
Please reply to
Mrs. John Daen Strong
241 Belville Place
Dayton, Ohio

TWENTY-FIFTH WEDDING ANNIVERSARY JUBILEE MASS

1940   1965
Mr. and Mrs. John Albert O'Connell
invite you to attend
the Jubilee Mass
Twenty-Fifth Anniversary
of their marriage
Thursday the twenty-second of May
at eleven o'clock
Saint James Catholic Church
Chicago
and afterwards at luncheon
Drake Hotel

SACRIFICIAL MASS FOR FIFTIETH WEDDING ANNIVERSARY

1915   1965
Mr. and Mrs. Albert O'Connell
request the honour of your presence
at the Holy Sacrifice of the Mass
on the occasion of their
Fiftieth Wedding Anniversary
at nine o'clock
Saint James Catholic Church
San Francisco, California

A card invitation to a breakfast is included with this invitation.

Breakfast
at ten o'clock
Three forty-five Country Lane
Please reply

THE BRIDE ISSUES HER OWN INVITATIONS

If the bride has no living relatives or close friends to issue her invitations, she may issue them herself and/or she may send her own announcements.

The young bride very seldom uses this method as it should not be used if there are parents, relatives, or friends to issue the invitations; but there may be circumstances when it is necessary.

The older bride very often issues her own invitations and announcements.

If the invitations are issued by the couple, the form is:

The honour of your presence
is requested at the marriage of
Miss Ellen Jane Fowler
to
Mr. Robert Charles Brown
on Friday, the fifteenth of June
at eight o'clock in the evening
First Methodist Church
Miami

Reception card form:

Reception
immediately following the ceremony
Park Plaza Hotel
Please reply to
2820 Lucerne Terrace

A RELATIVE ISSUES THE INVITATIONS

See Chapter 6, "Deceased Parents."

A FRIEND ISSUES THE INVITATIONS

See Chapter 6, "Deceased Parents."

BRIDE AND GROOM ISSUE OWN INVITATIONS

See Chapter 6, "Deceased Parents."

DOUBLE WEDDINGS

SISTERS

When the brides are sisters, the invitation reads the same as the traditional ceremony invitation except "daughter" would become "daughters" and the couple's names are linked by the word "and." Such as:

> *Nancy Jane*
> *to*
> *Mr. William Judd Bell*
> *and*
> *Mary Anne*
> *to*
> *Mr. Earl Noyes Miller*
> *etc.*

The elder daughter's name appears first on the invitation. Any other rules given would also apply to double ceremony and reception invitations.

WHEN THE BRIDES ARE NOT SISTERS

Here again "daughter" would become "daughters" and couple's names are linked by the word "and." Such as:

> *Mr. and Mrs. James Arthur Reid*
> *and*
> *The Reverend and Mrs. John Taylor Jones*
> *request the honour of your presence*
> *at the marriage of their daughters*
> *Nancy Jane Reid*
> *to*
> *Mr. William Judd Bell*
> *and*
> *Mary Anne Jones*
> *to*
> *Mr. Earl Noyes Miller*
> *Friday the eighth of June*
> *etc.*

The elder girl's name appears first on the invitation.

The last names of both girls are included in order to clarify the invitation.

Reception cards follow the usual form.

A reply to a double reception invitation when the brides are not sisters is sent to both couples issuing the invitation.

Individual invitations may be sent for a double wedding and reception if the parents wish to do so.

HOME WEDDINGS

WEDDING AND RECEPTION AT THE BRIDE'S HOME

All invitations to a home wedding carry an R.S.V.P. as preparations must be made for the number of guests attending.

Invitations to a home wedding may use "request the pleasure of your company" instead of "request the honour of your presence."

All guests who are invited to a home ceremony would naturally be invited to the home reception held afterwards, as no guest would be expected to leave before the reception.

If the home wedding is taking place in a very large city, the state need not be included in the invitation. The invitation form for a home ceremony and reception is:

> *Mr. and Mrs. James Arthur Reid*
> *request the pleasure of your company*
> *at the marriage of their daughter*
> *Nancy Jane*
> *to*
> *Mr. William Edward Pope*
> *on Saturday, the eighth of December*   ("on" may
>   be omitted)
> *One thousand nine hundred and sixty-five*   (year
> *at five o'clock*   may be
> *2400 Arlington Avenue*   omitted)
> *Atlanta*   (state may be omitted,
>   if large city)

The favour of a reply is requested

SMALL WEDDING, LARGE RECEPTION

A small home ceremony to which only the participants, relatives, and a few close friends are invited is often followed

by a larger home reception. Here the reception invitation
would appear upon the larger, double sheet. The smaller
enclosed card would be the invitation to the ceremony and
sent to only those few people invited to the ceremony and to
the reception. The form for the home reception is:

> *Mr. and Mrs. James Arthur Reid*
> *request the pleasure of your company*
> *at the wedding reception of their daughter*   (or
> *Nancy Jane*   breakfast)
> *and*   (take note)
> *Mr. William Edward Pope*
> *on Saturday, the eighth of December*
> *at six o'clock*
> *2400 Arlington Avenue*
> *Atlanta*
>
> *Kindly respond*

Form for ceremony card:

> *Mr. and Mrs. James Arthur Reid*
> *request the pleasure of your company*
> *at the marriage ceremony*
> *on Saturday, the eighth of December*
> *at five o'clock*
> *2400 Arlington Avenue*
> *Atlanta*

Or a small card with simply:

> *Ceremony at five o'clock*

If the home ceremony is going to be so small as to include
only relatives and a very few close friends, they may be
invited by word of mouth or by informal notes written by the
bride's mother; or the bride's mother may use a calling card
carrying the names of her and her husband. If informal notes
are written or calling cards are used, they are NOT enclosed
in the reception invitation but are mailed separately the same
day as the reception invitation or a day or two later.

If calling cards are used, the bride's mother writes at the
top of the card "Ceremony at five o'clock," such as:

> *Ceremony at five o'clock**
> *Mr. and Mrs. James Arthur Reid*

---

* Written by hand.

WEDDING AND RECEPTION AT FRIEND'S HOME

Even though a wedding is to be held at a friend's home, if the bride's parents are living, the invitations are issued in their name, whether they can attend or not. If the bride's parents are deceased, a near relative or friend may sponsor the bride.

If the bride's parents issue the invitations, they are worded the same as any other home ceremony invitation, such as:

> *Mr. and Mrs. James Arthur Reid*
> *request the pleasure of your company* (take note)
> *at the marriage of their daughter*
> *Nancy Jane*
> *to*
> *Mr. William Edward Pope*
> *Tuesday the first of May*
> *at three o'clock*
> *at the residence of Mr. and Mrs. Peter Lee Wright*
> *Twenty Rio Vista Lane* (written out when
> numbers are small)
> *Raleigh, North Carolina*

R.S.V.P.
245 Grace Street
(bride's address)

The replies to this invitation are sent to the address of the bride in order to save friends as much responsibility as possible.

If friends issue the invitation, the form is:

> *Mr. and Mrs. Peter Lee Wright*
> *request the pleasure of your company*
> *at the marriage of*
> *Miss Nancy Jane Reid*   (note Miss, and
> *to*   last name is used)
> *Mr. William Edward Pope*
> *on Saturday, the eighth of December* ("on"
> may be omitted)
> *One thousand nine hundred and sixty-five* (year may
> *at five o'clock*   be omitted)
> *Twenty Rio Vista Lane*
> *Raleigh, North Carolina*

R.S.V.P.
245 Grace Street
(bride's address)

"Miss" is used when not a relative, and the bride's last name is included.

Replies are sent to the bride's address in order to save the host and hostess as much responsibility as possible.

WEDDING AND RECEPTION AT THE HOME OF A RELATIVE

Doctor and Mrs. Charles Burden
request the pleasure of your company
at the marriage of their niece   (or granddaughter, etc.)
Nancy Jane Reid   (last name is used
to   and no "Miss"
Mr. William Edward Pope when a relative)
Saturday the eighth of December
One thousand nine hundred and sixty-five (year may
at five o'clock   be omitted)
2345 Springdale Road
Athens, Georgia

R.S.V.P.
245 Grace Street
(bride's address)

Even if the bride's last name is the same as the last name of the relative issuing the invitation (such as brother, uncle, etc.), it is included in the invitation. No "Miss" is included when a relative issues the invitation.

INVITATION FOR ADOPTED DAUGHTER

An invitation of an adopted daughter reads the same as any other invitation with no mention of the adoption. If the adopted daughter's surname is different from that of her parents, her surname is included in the invitation, as "Dorothy Jean Glass."

If the bride is the adopted daughter of a woman who has never been married, the form reads:

Miss Evelyn Judith Hall
requests the honour of your presence
at the marriage of her adopted daughter
etc.

WEDDING INVITATION OF THE YOUNG WIDOW

Usually a second marriage is quite small and engraved invitations are not sent, announcements being more suitable.

If engraved invitations are sent for the young widow's marriage, they are issued by the bride's parents and the general rules for wedding invitations are followed, as for any other marriage. If engraved invitations are sent, the form is:

> *Mr. and Mrs. Peter Julian Luke*
> *request the honour of your presence*
> *at the marriage of their adopted daughter*
> *Louise Luke Lewis*   ("Mrs." is not
> *to*   used, see text)
> *etc.*

The daughter's name appears as a combination of her maiden and married surnames. "Mrs." is not used as it is apparent the daughter has been married before since her name is different from that of her parents.

The title "Mrs." is used when a widow sends out the invitations in her own name. It would then read "Mrs. George Kenneth Lewis."

There are those who prefer to use "Louise Luke Lewis" when sending out their own invitations. If this is used, "Mrs." does not precede it.

The title "Mrs. Louise Anne Lewis" is never used.

When the young widow issues her own invitation, the form is:

> *The honour of your presence*
> *is requested at the marriage of*
> *Mrs. George Kenneth Lewis*
> *to*
> *etc.*

Mature Widow's Invitation

The mature widow very seldom issues engraved invitations. Friends are usually invited verbally or by notes handwritten by the bride. Announcements are often sent. If engraved invitations are sent, the form is:

> *The honour of your presence*
> *is requested at the marriage of*
> *Mrs. Thomas William Ives*
> *to*
> *etc.*

The mature widow uses her former husband's name, not "Mrs. Dorothy Ives."

Reception Card:

> *The pleasure of your company is requested*
> *Friday the fifth of January*
> *at half after three o'clock*
> *Brookhaven Club*
> *New Orleans*

THE MATURE BRIDE

When there are no living relatives, which is often the case if the bride is an older woman, the invitation may be issued by the couple themselves. The form is:

> *The honour of your presence*
> *is requested at the marriage of*
> *Miss Evelyn Margaret Sears*
> *to*
> *Mr. Charles Henry Corey*
> *etc.*

Reception card form:

> *The pleasure of your company is requested*
> *Friday the fifth of January*
> *at half after three o'clock*
> *Brookhaven Club*
> *New Orleans*

OVERSEAS BRIDE

Since very few friends and relatives would be able to attend the overseas bride's wedding, engraved announcements are usually sent by the bride's parents instead of invitations to the ceremony.

If engraved invitations are sent, they follow the usual form. See Chapter 7, "Announcements."

INVITATION OF THE YOUNG DIVORCEE

Very seldom are engraved invitations issued for the marriage of a divorcee. More properly, friends are invited by informal notes written by the bride's mother. Engraved announcements are often sent. If engraved invitations are sent, they are issued by the bride's parents, such as:

> *Mr. and Mrs. Melville Thomas Hoyt*
> *request the honour of your presence*
> *at the marriage of their daughter*
> *Hazel Hoyt Brown* (a combination of the
> *to*   bride's maiden and
> *etc.*   married surnames)

Reception card follows the usual form.

"Mrs." is not used on the invitation unless the bride sends out the invitations in her own name; her name would then be "Mrs. Hoyt Brown" never "Mrs. Hazel Brown."

If the young divorcee issues her own invitations, the form is:

> *The honour of your presence*
> *is requested at the marriage of*
> Mrs. Hoyt Brown (a combination of the
> to   bride's maiden and
> etc.   married surnames)

INVITATION OF THE OLDER DIVORCEE

Engraved wedding invitations are not sent for the older divorcee's marriage. Engraved announcements are often sent. See page 79.

THE REMARRIAGE OF DIVORCED PERSONS TO EACH OTHER

When a divorced couple remarry each other, no formal announcements are sent out. Friends and relatives are informed of this happy event by word of mouth, informal notes, or telegram. No formal announcement is released to the newspaper.

EMERGENCIES

BRIDE OR GROOM BECOMES ILL

If the bride or groom becomes seriously ill or is seriously injured a day or two before the ceremony, invitations are recalled by telephone or telegram. Notices are sent immediately to the newspaper.

DEATH IN THE IMMEDIATE FAMILY

If there is a death in the immediate family, the invitations may be recalled by telephone or telegram. If the deceased person has requested before death that the arrangements not be changed, the wedding may take place as originally scheduled. Notices are sent immediately to the newspaper in case of postponement.

In either of the above cases, if time permits, a handwritten note or a printed card may be sent. The form is:

> *Mr. and Mrs. Clarence Atwood Lloyd*
> *regret that owing to illness in the family*   (or a
>   *the invitation to*   death)
>   *their daughter's wedding*
>   *on Monday, the fourth of June*
>   *must be recalled*

If there has been a death in the family, wedding invitations issued to a large wedding may be recalled by telephone or telegram and the wedding may take place with just a few close friends and relatives of the bride and groom present.

ENGAGEMENT BROKEN AFTER INVITATIONS HAVE BEEN MAILED

If an engagement is broken after the invitations to the ceremony have been mailed and there is time before the date of the ceremony, engraved or printed notices are sent recalling the wedding invitations, such as:

> *Mr. and Mrs. Douglas John Tucker*
> *announce that the marriage of their daughter*
>   *Virginia*
>   *to*
>   *Mr. Miles Keith Asher*
>   *Will not take place*

If there is not time to send engraved or printed notices or to write notes with the same spacing as above on folded white note paper, the invited guests are notified by telegram or telephone. The telegram would be signed by those issuing the invitations and would read:

"The marriage of our daughter Virginia to Miles Kenneth Asher will not take place. Mr. and Mrs. Douglas John Tucker."

A telegram to a relative would be less formally worded.

No reason is given for the broken engagement.

POSTPONED WEDDING

If for some reason a wedding has been postponed but another date has been decided upon, guests may be informed by telegram or if there is time a new *printed* invitation may be sent, done in the same style as the first engraved invitation, such as:

Mr. and Mrs. Douglas John Tucker
announce that the marriage of their daughter
Virginia
to
Mr. Miles Keith Asher
has been postponed from
Saturday the tenth of April
until
Saturday the fifth of June
at five o'clock
First Methodist Church
Pittsburgh

Notices are sent to the newspaper immediately.
No reason is given for the postponement.

Returning Wedding Gifts

If a wedding does not take place, ALL wedding gifts must
be returned.

If a marriage is postponed, the wedding gifts are not returned unless the marriage still does not take place within a
reasonable length of time, in which case they are returned
with a thank-you note.

If a marriage lasts only a short time, the wedding gifts are
not returned unless the gifts have been unopened and unused, in which case it is better to return them, with a thank-
you note.

Handwritten Informal Invitations

If the wedding is being held at home or anywhere other
than a church with a limited number of friends invited, or if
it is to be a small church wedding, handwritten notes are
more in keeping than engraved invitations.

Handwritten invitations are written by the bride's mother;
or if she is deceased, the bride's father issues them. If he too
is deceased, a close relative (such as sister, brother, aunt,
grandmother), guardian, or close friend issues them. The
young bride may issue her own invitations if she has no close
relatives or friends to issue them for her. The mature bride
very often issues her own invitations. The widow or divorcee
very often issues her own informal invitations.

There is no strictly prescribed form for handwritten informal invitations. They read very much like any other informal invitation.

The paper used should be of the highest quality. Blue-black or black ink is used.

The informal or fold-over card, with or without name (or names), printed or engraved, may be used for issuing the informal invitation. An informal or fold-over card, with JOINT NAMES either printed or engraved, may be used for an informal invitation issued by the bride's parents (or grandparents, aunt and uncle, etc.). If the invitation is written on the inside of the informal or fold-over card, it is signed with the bride's mother's (grandmother's, aunt's, etc.) name only.

INFORMAL HANDWRITTEN INVITATION

Dear Florence (no punctuation)

Mary Martha and Robert Corey are being married at St. John's Chapel on Friday, March the tenth, at two o'clock. We hope you and George will be able to come to the ceremony, and afterwards to our home.

    Most sincerely (or Love, or Affectionately)
    Agnes Patersen (Agnes)

Very often engraved announcements are sent after the informal wedding; they are never sent to those who have been invited to the ceremony or the reception. See Chapter 7, "Announcements."

Handwritten invitations are sent two to three weeks before the ceremony.

TELEPHONED INVITATIONS

Quite often for the small wedding guests are invited by telephone. The bride's mother invites the guests (the bride may make the calls but she states that she is calling for her mother). If she is deceased, the bride's father or some close relative such as grandmother, aunt, or older sister, invites them. If the bride has no close relatives, she may invite the guests herself.

Chapter 5. Divorced Parents' Invitations

RULES FOR DIVORCED PARENTS ISSUING CEREMONY AND
RECEPTION INVITATIONS

Never under any circumstances may the names of both
divorced parents appear on the same ceremony invitation or
on the combination ceremony and reception invitation. Both
divorced parents' names may appear on an announcement of
a marriage. See page 77.

If one divorced parent issues the ceremony invitation and
the other parent issues the reception invitation, separate invitations are sent.

If either divorced parent has remarried and that parent is
issuing the reception invitation, the name of the stepmother
or stepfather MUST appear on the invitation, as the stepparent
is the host with the real parent.

If a mother is divorced and remarried and she is issuing
her daughter's ceremony invitations, the daughter's last name
is included as the names would now be different, such as:
Mary Elizabeth Johnson.

If the bride's mother is issuing the ceremony or reception
invitations and she has not remarried, she uses a combination
of her married and maiden surnames on the invitation such
as:

Mrs. Cullen Roberts   (Cullen being her
maiden name)

She would never use Mrs. Louise Roberts.

If it is less awkward for her, a remarried mother may issue her daughter's invitations in her name only, such as:

> Mrs. Ralph Allen Carter
> *requests the honour of your presence*
> *at the marriage of her daughter*
> Mary Elizabeth Johnson   (daughter's last
> *etc.*   name is included)

1 ... MOTHER AND FATHER DIVORCED—FATHER NOT REMARRIED, MOTHER NOT REMARRIED

A ... Daughter is living with mother

In this case the bride's mother issues the ceremony invitations. If a friendly attitude prevails, the father may issue the reception invitations; if it does not, the bride's mother would issue these also.

The bride's mother uses a combination of her maiden and married surnames, such as:

> Mrs. Cullen Roberts   (Cullen being her
>   maiden name)
> *requests the honour of your presence*
> *at the marriage of her daughter*
> Cynthia Anne
> *etc.*

If the bride's mother is issuing the reception invitations, any of the traditional forms may be used, or she may use the combination ceremony and reception invitation. See page 41.

If the bride's father is issuing the reception invitations, the traditional form may be used and mailed separately by the father.

B ... Daughter is living with father

In this case the father issues the ceremony invitations.

The mother may issue the reception invitations using the traditional form and mailing separately. See page 41.

If the father is also issuing the reception invitations, he may use any of the traditional forms or the combination ceremony and reception invitation. See page 42.

The form for the father's ceremony invitation is:

> *Mr. Richard Skyler Roberts*
> *requests the honour of your presence*
> *at the marriage of his daughter*
> *Cynthia Anne*
> *etc.*

2 . . . MOTHER AND FATHER DIVORCED—MOTHER REMARRIED,
FATHER NOT REMARRIED

A . . . Daughter is living with mother

The bride's mother may issue the ceremony and reception invitations with her present husband; or if it is less awkward, she may issue the ceremony invitations alone. The reception invitations, however, must include the name of the stepfather, as he is the host with the real mother.

If the mother has recently remarried, the following form may be used:

> *Mr. and Mrs. Allen Ralph Scott*
> *request the honour of your presence*
> *at the marriage of Mrs. Scott's daughter*
> *Cynthia Anne Roberts*   (last name is
> *etc.*   included)

Or if the bride has lived in the home of her stepfather since childhood and has little or no contact with her real father, the following form may be used:

> *Mr. and Mrs. Allen Ralph Scott*
> *request the honour of your presence*
> *at the marriage of their daughter*
> *Cynthia Anne Roberts*   (last name is
> *etc.*   included)

If the bride's mother and the stepfather also give the reception, the reception invitation MUST be issued by the mother AND the stepfather, as he is the host with his wife. Any of the traditional reception forms may be used and enclosed in the ceremony invitation, or the combination ceremony and reception form may be used. See page 42.

If the bride's real father gives the reception, the traditional reception form is used and mailed separately by the father.

B . . . Daughter is living with father

The father may issue the ceremony and reception invitations, unless a friendly attitude prevails and all agree that the mother will issue the ceremony invitations, either in her name or with her present husband. The reception invitations may be issued by the father or by the mother AND the stepfather.

If the father is giving the wedding and the reception he uses the traditional form, or he may use the combination ceremony and reception form. See page 42.

> *Mr. Richard Skyler Roberts*
> *requests the honour of your presence*
> *at the marriage of his daughter*
> > *Cynthia Anne* (last name not included)
> > *etc.*

If the mother and the stepfather give the reception, the invitations MUST be issued in both their names, as the stepfather is the host with his wife. Their reception invitations are mailed separately by them. Traditional reception form is used. See page 41.

3...MOTHER AND FATHER DIVORCED—MOTHER NOT REMARRIED, FATHER REMARRIED

A . . . Daughter is living with mother

The mother would issue the ceremony invitations. The form is:

> > *Mrs. Cullen Roberts* (a combination of
> > > her maiden and
> > > married surnames)
> > *requests the honour of your presence*
> > *at the marriage of her daughter*
> > > *Cynthia Anne* (last name is not used)
> > > *etc.*

The bride's mother may use the traditional reception invitation form (in her name only, Mrs. Cullen Roberts), or she may use the combination reception and ceremony invitation form. See page 42.

If the real father and the stepmother issue the reception invitations, they MUST be issued in his name and that of his present wife, as she is the hostess for the occasion. Their reception invitations are mailed separately by them.

B . . . Daughter is living with father and stepmother

Father may issue the ceremony invitations in his name using this form:

> *Mr. Richard Skyler Roberts*
> *requests the honour of your presence*
> *at the marriage of his daughter*
> > *Cynthia Anne*   (last name is not used)
> > *etc.*

Or if the bride has lived in the home of her father and stepmother since childhood, the form may be:

> *Mr. and Mrs. Richard Skyler Roberts*
> *request the honour of your presence*
> *at the marriage of their daughter*
> > *Cynthia Anne*   (last name is not used)
> > *etc.*

If the bride's real father and stepmother give the reception also, the reception invitation MUST be issued by the father AND stepmother, as she is the hostess for the occasion. The traditional reception card may be used and enclosed in the ceremony invitation, or the combination ceremony and reception invitation may be used. See Chapter 4.

If the real mother is giving the reception, the reception invitation is issued in her name (Mrs. Cullen Roberts, a combination of her maiden and married surnames) and mailed separately by her. The traditional form may be used. See Chapter 4.

4 . . . MOTHER AND FATHER DIVORCED—MOTHER REMARRIED, FATHER REMARRIED

A . . . Daughter is living with mother and stepfather

Ceremony and reception forms and rules would be the same as for 2 . . . A.

B . . . Daughter is living with father and stepmother

Ceremony and reception forms and rules would be the same as for 3 . . . B.

ANNOUNCEMENTS FOR DIVORCED PARENTS

See page 76.

DIVORCED PARENTS AT THE WEDDING AND RECEPTION

MOTHER GIVING THE WEDDING

Even if a divorced mother gives her daughter's wedding, the real father may give the bride away, calling for her at the mother's home in the bridal car. If the real father does not give the bride away, some other male member of the family may, either brother, uncle, grandfather, etc., or the mother may have this privilege if there is no male member of the family available.

If the mother gives the wedding, she takes her place in the front row of the church (with or without her present husband). If relations are strained, it might be better if the mother's present husband did not attend the ceremony.

The real father after giving the bride away takes his place a few rows behind the real mother, with or without (if relations are strained) his present wife.

Ushers should be notified of the seating arrangement for the parents.

If the bride has been raised by her stepfather, has had little or no contact with her real father, and looks upon the stepfather as her real father, he of course gives the bride away.

MOTHER GIVING THE RECEPTION

If the mother has not remarried, she receives the guests alone; or she may ask a male relative to receive with her. If the mother has remarried, her present husband receives with her, no matter what the relations are between the bride and her stepfather.

The bride's real father may go to the reception; and if relations are friendly, he may be accompanied by his wife. He goes merely as a guest, however, and takes no part in the receiving of the guests.

Whether a mother or a father goes to a reception hosted by the ex-spouse's second wife or husband depends entirely upon the circumstances involved. Very difficult situations can arise at weddings given by divorced parents; but if each parent and stepparent can remember that this should be the happiest day of their child's life, they will put aside their personal feelings to make it such.

FATHER GIVING THE WEDDING

It is very rare for a divorced and remarried father to give his daughter's wedding if the real mother is still living. It is by far the best plan for the mother to give the daughter's wedding, even if the wedding she can afford might be very plain and simple compared to one the real father, who might be wealthy, could afford.

There are instances when a divorced and remarried father gives his daughter's wedding, such as if the father remarried when the daughter was very young and the stepmother raised his daughter from childhood with little or no interest shown by the real mother. Surely in a case like this the real mother could not expect to give her daughter's wedding, nor should the stepmother be expected to sit anywhere in the church but beside her husband in the front pew.

If for some reason the real father does give his daughter's wedding (and circumstances are not out of the ordinary, as evidenced by the above mentioned case), the real mother takes her place in the front row of the church with (or without) her present husband.

Ushers are notified of the seating arrangement.

FATHER GIVING THE RECEPTION

Many times when a couple is divorced the real mother will give the wedding and the real father will give the reception.

If the father has remarried, his present wife is the hostess and she stands in the receiving line with the father.

The real mother may attend the reception with (or without) her present husband; but if the real father has remarried, the real mother can take no active part in receiving the guests. If the real father has not remarried, the real mother may stand in the receiving line with her former husband in his home, whether she has remarried or not. In this case the real father is the first in the receiving line to greet the guests.

In case the real mother has remarried, her present husband may attend the reception as a guest.

SEPARATED PARENTS

Separated parents may issue joint invitations and announcements for their daughter's wedding, and they may take the usual part in the ceremony and the reception.

If the separated parents do not want to issue joint invitations or announcements, they are issued by the parent with whom the daughter makes her home, which would usually be the mother. If the bride's mother issues the invitations, she uses her husband's name, such as:

> *Mrs. William Towle* (not Mrs. Mary Anne
> Towle or Mrs. Smith Towle)

Chapter 6. Deceased Parents

BOTH PARENTS DECEASED

When a bride's parents are both deceased, her wedding invitations or announcements are issued by a relative or close friend. Occasionally a young bride and groom with no close relatives or friends will issue their own invitations and announcements.

Grandparents issue the invitations

> *Mr. and Mrs. Robert Townes*   (if one grandparent, Mr. or Mrs.)
>
> *request the honour of your presence*
> *at the marriage of their granddaughter*   (if one grandparent, his or her)
>
> *Charlotte Louise Harris*   (last name is
> *etc.*   included)

70

Unmarried brother, sister, aunt, or uncle issues the invitations

Mr. Robert Alvin Townes   (or Miss Mary
Anne Townes)
(or if maternal aunt,
Miss Jean Ann Nye)
requests the honour of your presence
at the marriage of his sister   (or her sister,
her niece, his niece)
Charlotte Louise Townes   (last name is
etc.   included)

Married brother or uncle issues the invitations

Mr. and Mrs. Robert Alvin Townes
request the honour of your presence
at the marriage of their sister (or their niece,
his sister,
his niece)
Charlotte Louise Townes   (last name is
etc.   included)

Married sister or married aunt issues the invitations

Mr. and Mrs. Albert Lewis Brown
request the honour of your presence
at the marriage of their sister (or their niece,
her sister, her niece)
Charlotte Louise Townes   (last name is
etc.   included)

If an invitation or announcement is issued by a close relative (sister, brother, aunt, uncle, grandparent), the relationship is shown in the invitation. The connection is not shown
if the invitation is issued by friends, cousins, guardians, etc.

Even if the bride's last name is the same as the last name
of the relative issuing the invitation (brother, unmarried
sister, etc.), it is included in the invitation. No "Miss" is included when a relative issues the invitation.

Reception invitation forms

Any of the traditional reception forms may be used with
the ceremony invitation. Since no reception invitation makes
any mention of the bride's name, no relationship would have
to be shown.

If the combination ceremony and reception invitation is

used, the relationship shown would be the same as in the
ceremony invitation.

Announcements

Announcements made by any of the above show the same
relationship as the ceremony invitation. The traditional announcement form is used, and the same rules are followed as
for any other announcement. See page 76.

Bride and groom issue own invitations

Very often the mature bride and groom issue their own
invitations and announcements; or if the young bride has no
close relatives or friends, she and her groom may issue them
together. The form is:

> *The honour of your presence*
> *is requested at the marriage of*
> *Miss Charlotte Louise Townes*   ("Miss" is
> *to*   used here)
> *Mr. Thomas Arthur Beard*
> *etc.*

Reception form:

> *The pleasure of your company*
> *is requested at the wedding reception of*
> *Miss Charlotte Louise Townes*   ("Miss" is
> *etc.*   used)

or:

> *The pleasure of your company is requested*
> *Friday the tenth of May*
> *at four o'clock*
> *The Deauville*
> *Charlotte, North Carolina*
> *Please send reply to*
> *78 Springdale Road*

A friend issues the invitations

> *Mr. and Mrs. Frederick Lee Holloman*
> *request the honour of your presence*
> *at the marriage of*
> *Miss Charlotte Louise Harris*   ("Miss" is
> *etc.*   always used
>   when friends
>   issue the
>   invitations)

WEDDING INVITATION WHEN ONE PARENT IS DECEASED

When one parent is deceased, the wedding invitations or announcements are issued by the living parent.

If the mother is deceased and the father has remarried, the invitations may read exactly like the invitations issued by both real parents, as the names would all be the same.

If the mother is deceased and the father has recently remarried or if there is no mother-daughter relationship, the invitations may read:

> *Mr. and Mrs. Arnold Burton Robbins*
> *request the honour of your presence*
> *at the marriage of Mr. Robbins' daughter*
> *Marjorie Catherine*
> *etc.*

If the father is deceased and the mother has remarried, the invitation may read:

> *Mr. and Mrs. Gregory James Whitfield*
> *request the honour of your presence*
> *at the marriage of their daughter*
> (or her daughter,
> or Mrs. Whitfield's
> daughter)
>
> *Shirley Jane Meyer*   (last name is
> *to*   included)
> *etc.*

or:

Sometimes the invitations are issued by the remarried mother in her name only:

> *Mrs. Gregory James Whitfield*
> *requests the honour of your presence*
> *at the marriage of her daughter*
> *Shirley Jane Meyer*   (last name is
> *to*   included)
> *etc.*

RECEPTION INVITATION WHEN ONE PARENT IS DECEASED

When one parent is deceased, the reception invitations are issued by the living parent. If the living parent has remarried, the reception invitations are issued in conjunction with the stepparent.

If the larger combination ceremony and reception invitation is being used, where the daughter's name is mentioned, the relationship shown would be the same as that shown in the ceremony invitation (see page 73).

If there is a stepparent, he or she is the host or the hostess with the real parent, and his/her name MUST be included in any type reception invitation issued.

IF THE BRIDE'S MOTHER HAS RECENTLY REMARRIED

In case the bride's mother has recently remarried or if for some reason the bride prefers that her stepfather's name does not appear upon the ceremony invitations, the invitations may be issued in the name of the bride's mother only. But if a reception invitation is issued, it MUST contain the name of the stepfather, as he is the host with his wife.

If the invitations are issued by the bride's mother only, it could be interpreted as a slight and might indicate that the bride and her stepfather are not on friendly terms. If this is not the case, it is best to issue the ceremony invitations in both names.

FATHER DECEASED, MOTHER HAS NOT REMARRIED —WHO GIVES THE BRIDE AWAY?

If the bride's father is deceased and her mother has not remarried, a close male relative (a brother, uncle, grandfather, etc.) gives her away. If there is no close male relative, the bride's mother may give her away.

MOTHER DECEASED, FATHER HAS NOT REMARRIED —WHO RECEIVES AT THE RECEPTION?

If the bride's mother is deceased and her father has not remarried, the father may invite a close female relative or close friend to receive with him at the reception and act as hostess for the occasion. The father is the first in line to greet the guests, however. If there is a female relative living in the bride's home, such as an aunt or grandmother, she would take the place of the mother of the bride and be the first in line to greet the guests.

If the father has remarried, his present wife is the hostess with him.

Chapter 7. Announcements

Even though there have been wedding and reception invitations, there may still be a list to whom announcements should be sent, especially to out-of-town relatives and friends who might not otherwise hear of the marriage.

Many people send announcements especially to out-of-town relatives and friends because they feel they want to inform these relatives and friends of the marriage, but they do not want them to think they are requesting a wedding gift. Actually NO type of invitation requires a wedding gift, but it seems to be understood by more people that an announcement does not require one.

Announcements are frequently used to tell of a quiet wedding which only members of the family have attended or to tell of a wedding that has already taken place.

Announcements are NEVER sent to those who have been invited to the wedding or to the reception.

"At home" cards may be included in announcements.

Announcements ALWAYS include the day, month, and year that the ceremony took place.

Announcements ALWAYS include the name of the city and state where the ceremony took place.

The procedure for addressing announcements is the same as for addressing invitations. See Chapter 12.

The traditional announcement follows the same form as the traditional wedding invitation, except that the wording is changed a little.

Nothing but engraved announcements may be sent for a formal wedding or for a wedding held in a church.

TRADITIONAL ANNOUNCEMENT FORM

> *Mr. and Mrs. Henry John Melville*
> *announce the marriage of their daughter*
> > (or have the honour to
> > announce, or have the
> > honour of announcing)
>
> *Lucy Josephine*
> *to*
> *Mr. Kendrick Walter Carpenter*
> *on Friday, the first of June* (date must be
> > mentioned)
> *One thousand nine hundred and sixty-five*
> > (year must be included)
> *Saint Luke's Cathedral*
> > (optional whether place
> > is included)
> *Palm Springs, California*
> > (city and state must be
> > included)

WHEN ANNOUNCEMENTS ARE MAILED

Announcements are mailed the day of the wedding (after the ceremony) or as soon after the ceremony as possible. Announcements are mailed by the bride's parents from the city in which they reside.

THE GROOM'S PARENTS AND THE MARRIAGE ANNOUNCEMENT

The groom's parents never formally announce their son's marriage.

DIVORCED PARENTS MAKING ANNOUNCEMENT

The position of the divorced parent is the same in the wedding announcement as in the wedding invitation. The announcement of a marriage is usually made by the parent with whom the daughter lives, with the same variations as in the wedding invitation. See Chapter 5, "Divorced Parents' Invitations."

Certain circumstances may make it expedient for one parent to announce the marriage of a daughter without mentioning the other parent, although this is not customary procedure. One circumstance might be when the bride-to-be has been legally adopted by her stepfather and she bears his name and has had little or no contact with her real father. In this case the mother and the stepfather make the announcement jointly with no mention of the real father. Both divorced parents may announce their daughter's marriage together, a much better procedure than omitting one parent's name from the wedding announcement. Although this was frowned upon years ago, time changes many things. This solution to a delicate problem is much better and is certainly less embarrassing for the daughter, who after all is the person to be considered.

On the wedding invitation the names of both divorced parents may NEVER appear on the same invitation, but on the announcement of a marriage they may and the reason is apparent.

Divorced parents' announcement form:

> *Mrs. Charles Richard Wade* (mother's name
> *Mr. Anthony Lynn Buckmaster* appears first)
> *announce the marriage of their daughter*
> *Helen Grace*
> *to*
> *Mr. James William Kennedy*
> *Wednesday the second of January* (date must
> be included)
> *One thousand nine hundred and sixty-five* (year
> must be included)
> *Saint Christopher's Cathedral* (optional
> whether place is mentioned)
> *Davenport, Iowa* (city and state must
> be included)

DIVORCED MOTHER'S NAME

If a divorced mother has not remarried, she uses the combination of her maiden and married surnames, such as: Mrs. Jones Smith.

If the divorced mother has remarried, she uses her present husband's name.

DIVORCED GROOM

The fact that the groom has been divorced has no effect whatsoever upon the announcement of his new marriage.

WEDDING ANNOUNCEMENT OF ADOPTED DAUGHTER

Announcements are sent by the adopted daughter's mother and father, or mother or father alone if either is deceased, the same as for any other announcement.

If the bride is the adopted daughter of a woman who has never married, the form is:

> *Miss Evelyn Judith Hall*
> *has the honour of announcing*
> *the marriage of her adopted daughter*
> *etc.*

BRIDE AND GROOM MAKE THEIR OWN ANNOUNCEMENT

Announcements may be issued by the principals in the wedding, especially if the bride is mature or if the young bride has no close relatives or friends to make the announcement for her. "At Home" information may appear upon this type of announcement.

Form:

> *Miss Charlotte Elizabeth Harris*
> *and*
> *Mr. Russell Stephen Davis*
> *announce their marriage*
> *Wednesday the sixteenth of May*
> *One thousand nine hundred and sixty-five*
> *Athens, Georgia*
> *After the third of June*
> *171 Grove Park, Athens*

ANNOUNCEMENT OF THE WIDOW

If the bride is a young widow, her announcement is made by her parents exactly as was the announcement of her first marriage, except now her deceased husband's name is included.

If the parents make the young widow's announcement, the form is:

> *Mr. and Mrs. Charles Richard Harris*
> *announce the marriage of their daughter*
>   *Charlotte Harris Davis* (the bride's maiden
>   *etc.*   and married surnames)

If the young or mature widow issues her own announcement, the form is:

>   *Mrs. Russell Stephen Davis*   (former hus-
>   *and*   band's name)
>   *Doctor Marvin Lee Folsom*
>   *announce their marriage*
>   *etc.*

If the mature widow has been known in the business world by her maiden and married surnames, she may use this combination on her announcement: Mrs. Harris Davis.

ANNOUNCEMENT OF THE DIVORCEE

The young divorcee's parents usually issue their daughter's announcements. The form is:

> *Mr. and Mrs. Charles Richard Harris*
> *have the honour of announcing*
> *the marriage of their daughter*
>   *Charlotte Harris Davis* (bride's maiden
>   *etc.*   name and her
>   former husband's
>   surname)

The more mature divorcee and her husband issue their own announcements. The form is:

>   *Mrs. Brown Sessions* (the combination of
>   *and*   her maiden and
>   *Mr. Grady Wilson*   married surnames)
>   *announce their marriage*
>   *etc.*

ANNOUNCEMENT AFTER ELOPEMENT

Many times announcements are not sent after an elopement, especially if the marriage has been kept secret for several months. If the parents have been told within a reasonable length of time, announcements may be sent. No reference is made to the elopement.

The announcements must include the city, state, day, month, and year of the ceremony. The form is the same as for any other announcement.

The bride's parents may entertain for the couple. Invitations issued to a party or reception are mailed separately. They are never enclosed in the announcement envelope.

Many times and for many reasons marriages are performed by someone other than a minister. Occasionally a couple would like to receive the blessings of the church. This is a problem that must be discussed with their minister. If he gives his approval and their marriage is blessed, the following card may be enclosed with the announcement of their marriage:

> *Mr. and Mrs. Richard Evans Johnson*
> *received the Blessings of the Church upon their marriage*
> *Saturday the first of May*
> *Saint John's Church*
> *Toledo, Ohio*

THE REMARRIAGE OF A DIVORCED COUPLE TO EACH OTHER

If a couple who has been divorced remarry each other, no formal announcement is made of their remarriage; the news is told to friends by word of mouth or by letter. No announcement is sent to the newspaper.

A RELATIVE ISSUES THE ANNOUNCEMENT

The relationship shown is the same as for wedding invitations. See Chapter 6, "Deceased Parents."

A FRIEND ISSUES THE ANNOUNCEMENT

The relationship is the same as for wedding invitations. See Chapter 6, "Deceased Parents."

DOUBLE WEDDING ANNOUNCEMENT

If the brides are sisters, a joint announcement is sent.

If the brides are not sisters, separate announcements of each marriage are sent.

SEPARATED PARENTS

Separated parents may issue joint announcements. The form is the same as for any other announcement.

Chapter 8. Enclosure Cards

CHURCH ADMISSION CARDS

These cards are used for large and fashionable weddings of such great public interest that uninvited guests might appear in numbers, leaving few seats for invited guests. At such weddings, church admission cards are used to insure seats for the invited guests. The church is closed to the public for the period of the ceremony, and only guests who present these cards are admitted.

The church admission card is engraved and enclosed with the ceremony invitation. The form is:

> *Please present this card*
> *at Saint John's Church*
> *Thursday the second of June*

PEW CARDS

It would be most unusual if pew cards were sent for the entire seating arrangement of the church, as many invited guests are unable to attend the ceremony, and the whole scheme of seating would have to be rearranged. More often they are used to assure members of the immediate families and honored guests seats in the front of the church. The first few pews on each side of the aisle are reserved for these guests, the left side for the bride's relatives and honored guests, the right side for the groom's relatives and honored guests.

81

Engraved pew cards may be enclosed in the ceremony invitation, but it is much more efficient to mail them after it has been determined who will be able to attend the ceremony.

Pew cards to match the invitations may be engraved and ordered at the same time as the invitations, or the engraver may carry them in his regular stock.

Pew cards differ from within-the-ribbon cards in that here a particular seat is assigned each guest.

Very often the bride's mother and the groom's mother send their own personal visiting cards for their sides of the church with the pew number handwritten in black ink in the lower left hand corner; or the bride's mother may send their cards for both, with the aid of the groom's mother.

Personal visiting card form

For the bride's side:

> *Bride's Reserved Section**
> *Mrs. Anthony Lee Avery*
> *Pew No. 10**

For the groom's side:

> *Groom's Reserved Section**
> *Mrs. Thomas Owen Vance*
> *Pew No. 35**

Engraved or stock pew cards are worded exactly like the church admission cards, with the pew number added. The form for stock pew card is:

> *Mr. and Mrs. Edwin Ralph Jones**
> *will present this card to an usher*
> *at*
> *Saint Luke's Cathedral*
> *Pew Number*
> *12**

Form for engraved pew card:

> *Mr. and Mrs. Edwin Ralph Jones**
> *will present this card to an usher*
> *at St. Luke's Cathedral*
> *Pew Number*
> *12**

* Written by hand.

WITHIN-THE-RIBBONS OR BRIDE'S RESERVED SECTION

Instead of assigning specific seats to the honored guests and members of the immediate families as in pew cards, the first few rows of seats in the front of the church, on either side, are reserved for these guests; and, with the exception of the mother and very close relatives who have their own special seats, guests are seated in this section according to their arrival at the church.

Within-the-ribbon cards may be sent for this section; they may be enclosed in the ceremony invitation, but it is more efficient to send them after it has been determined who will be able to attend the ceremony.

Here, as always, the right side of the church is for the groom's relatives and honored guests, the left side for the bride's.

If engraved cards are not being used, the bride's mother and the groom's mother may send their own personal visiting cards for their own sides of the church; or the bride's mother may send their cards for both sides, with the aid of the groom's mother.

Personal visiting card form

For the bride's side:

> *Bride's Reserved Section**
> *Mrs. Anthony Lee Avery*

For the groom's side:

> *Groom's Reserved Section**
> *Mrs. Thomas Owen Vance*

Engraved card form:

> *Please present this card*
> *at Saint Luke's Cathedral*
> *Tuesday the first day of May*
> *Bride's (or Groom's) Reserved Section**

Or:

> *Mr. and Mrs. Stanley Reid Morris**
> *will present this card to an usher*
> *at Saint Luke's Cathedral*
> *Tuesday the first day of May*
> *Bride's (or Groom's) Reserved Section**

---

* Written by hand.

If the number of guests to be invited to sit in this section is not too many, the bride's mother may invite them by telephone or word of mouth.

AT HOME CARDS

"At Home" cards may be sent with either ceremony and reception invitations or with announcements; they are sent more often with announcements, however. These engraved cards inform the receiver of the young couple's new address and the date when they will be at home to receive visitors. The form is:

> *At home*
> *after the tenth of June*
> *3500 Markum Avenue*
> *Little Rock, Arkansas*

"At Home" cards enclosed with the wedding invitation do not include the name of the couple.

It is incorrect to have "At Home" information engraved upon the wedding invitation.

"At Home" information may appear upon an announcement of a marriage made by the principals in the wedding. See "Bride and Groom Make Their Own Announcement," p. 78.

TRAIN CARDS

Sometimes train cards are used for very large weddings where guests can board a train at a special point to and from the wedding. A reserved car may be used for this, and the train card is presented to the conductor in lieu of a ticket.

An engraved train card matching the invitation may be enclosed in the ceremony invitation sent to those out-of-town guests that are expected, or it may be sent after the acceptance has been received. The form is:

> A special car will be attached to Seaboard Airline Train Number Five, leaving Miami at five o'clock June fifth. Returning train will leave New York, Pennsylvania Station, Sunday June tenth at three o'clock. Please present this card in place of ticket.

MAPS

Sometimes for the suburban or country wedding a map is reproduced on the same stock as the invitation and enclosed with it. These maps are of great assistance to guests coming by automobile.

If a rustic type map is used on a different stock from the invitation, it is mailed separately.

REPLY CARDS

It is not correct to enclose a reply card with a ceremony invitation, as this invitation needs no reply.

A matching reply card may be enclosed with the reception invitation, although an R.S.V.P. is more often engraved on the invitation itself. The form is:

Please send response to
1190 Arbor Lane
Raleigh, North Carolina

Chapter 9. Military Invitations and Announcements

THE FATHER OF THE BRIDE

The bride's father uses his rank with "and Mrs." on the first line of the invitation or announcement, whatever that rank may be.

UNITED STATES ARMY

If the groom holds the rank of Captain or above, his title precedes his name. The line following shows his Service designation, such as:

Captain William Henry Turner
United States Army

If the groom holds a rank below that of Captain, his name appears on a single line. The line following shows his title and "United States Army," such as:

William Henry Turner
Second Lieutenant, United States Army

If the groom holds the rank of Sergeant, the form is:

William Henry Turner
Sergeant, United States Army

NOTE: A member of a graduating class at Annapolis, West Point, or the United States Air Academy, to be married immediately following his commissioning, may have his rank shown on the wedding invitation even though the invitation is mailed before he is actually commissioned.

Below the rank of Sergeant, the form is:

> *William Henry Turner*   (no Mr.)
> *United States Army*

United States Air Force

If the groom is an officer or a noncommissioned officer in the Air Force, his name is prefaced by his title or rank. The line following shows his Service designation, such as:

> *Lieutenant William Henry Turner*
> *United States Air Force*

Or:

> *Colonel William Henry Turner*
> *Medical Corps, United States Air Force*

Below the rank of Sergeant the form is:

> *William Henry Turner*   (no Mr.)
> *United States Air Force*

United States Navy

If the groom holds the rank of Commander or higher, his rank precedes his name. The line following shows his Navy service, such as:

> *Commodore William Henry Turner*
> *United States Navy*

Or:

> *Captain William Henry Turner*
> *Medical Corps, United States Navy*

If the groom holds a rank below that of Commander, his name appears on a single line. The line following shows his rank and the Service:

> *William Henry Turner*
> *Lieutenant, junior grade, United States Navy*

If the groom holds no rank:

> *William Henry Turner*   (no Mr.)
> *United States Navy*

UNITED STATES MARINE CORPS

If the groom holds the rank of Major or above, his rank precedes his name. The line following shows his Service designation, such as:

Lieutenant Colonel William Henry Turner
United States Marine Corps

If the groom holds a rank below that of Major, his name appears on a single line. The following line shows his rank with the Service designation. "First" and "Second" Lieutenants are designated as such:

William Henry Turner
First Lieutenant, United States Marine Corps

Below the rank of Sergeant the form is:

William Henry Turner
United States Marine Corps

UNITED STATES ARMY RESERVE

If a Reserve Officer is on ACTIVE duty, the form is:

Captain William Henry Turner
United States Army

A Reserve Officer NOT on active duty, with rank of Captain or higher:

Major William Henry Turner
United States Army Reserve

A Reserve Officer NOT on active duty, with rank lower than that of Captain:

William Henry Turner
Lieutenant, United States Army Reserve

UNITED STATES AIR FORCE RESERVE

A Reserve Officer on ACTIVE duty:

Colonel William Henry Turner
United States Air Force

A Reserve Officer NOT on active duty:

Lieutenant William Henry Turner
United States Air Force Reserve

UNITED STATES NAVAL RESERVE

A Reserve Officer on ACTIVE duty:

Captain William Henry Turner
United States Naval Reserve

A Reserve Officer NOT on active duty uses the same form as a civilian.

UNITED STATES MARINE CORPS RESERVE

A Reserve Officer on ACTIVE duty, with rank of Major or higher:

Major William Henry Turner
United States Marine Corps Reserve

Below the rank of Major:

William Henry Turner
Captain, United States Marine Corps Reserve

A Reserve Officer uses the above forms whether or not he may be on active duty.

R.O.T.C. AND N.R.O.T.C. REGULATIONS PERTINENT TO WEDDINGS

A new Reserve Officer receiving a commission and awaiting the commencement of his obligated training tour is not entitled to use his rank and branch designation on wedding invitations or to have a military wedding in uniform.

This regulation pertains to the period between graduation and the assignment to active duty, which may be several weeks or months thereafter.

He may properly be identified, however, by rank and branch designation if as a new Reserve Officer he is "in fact" on active duty at the time of the wedding.

EXCEPTIONS

The engraving of rank and branch designation on the wedding invitation and the military wedding are completely proper if the wedding takes place at a church or chapel adjacent to or part of the college and immediately follows college graduation exercises.

The Air Force regulations for men in a Reserve status permit a military wedding and the use of the rank and branch designation on wedding invitations during the interim civilian period between graduation and the date of the training tour of duty. This does not pertain to graduates of Annapolis, West Point, or The Air Academy, as they are officers of a regular component.

RETIRED OFFICERS

Retired high ranking officers retain their titles in civilian life, such as:

> *Major General William Henry Turner*
> *United States Army, Retired*

THE BRIDE IN MILITARY SERVICE

If the bride and the groom are issuing their own invitations, she may use her military title. If the bride's parents issue the invitations, her title does not necessarily appear.

ABBREVIATIONS

No abbreviations of title or rank are allowed. A second given name may be omitted if title and name are very lengthy.

A hyphen is not used if the title has two words, such as Lieutenant Colonel, etc.

Junior is written out in full as "junior."

The title "Lieutenant, junior grade, United States Navy" is so written.

If the groom is a Second Lieutenant his full title is used.

ADDRESSING INVITATIONS

Explained in Chapter 12, "Addressing Invitations and Announcements."

Chapter 10. Acceptances and Regrets

If an invitation is for the church ceremony ONLY, it does not require an answer.

Any reception invitation, whether it is an invitation to the reception only or a combination ceremony and reception invitation, MUST be answered.

Replies to a formal reception invitation are sent in the formal traditional style in which they are extended.

Replies are written in longhand, in formal language, spaced correctly, on a folded sheet of fine quality note paper, in blue-black or black ink.

Informals or the fold-over card, with or without name engraved, are NOT used for an answer to a formal invitation. They may be used for an answer to an informal wedding or reception invitation.

The reply and the envelope are addressed to the name or names that appear upon the invitation.

A reply is always sent to a home ceremony invitation, as it would include a reception or breakfast afterwards and plans must be made.

If more than one invitation is received within a family, EACH is answered separately.

Replies are sent immediately after receiving the invitation.

THE FORMAL ACCEPTANCE

Mr. and Mrs. Dwight Charles Rich   (full name,
accept with pleasure   no initials)
Doctor and Mrs. Arthur John McLendon's (name as
it appears on the invitation)
kind invitation
for their daughter's wedding reception
Saturday the eighth of May
at four o'clock
Parkway Country Club*

Or:

Mr. and Mrs. Dwight Charles Rich   (full name,
accept with pleasure   no initials)
the kind invitation of
Doctor and Mrs. Arthur John McLendon (fullname
as it appears on the invitation)
to the wedding reception of their daughter
Shirley Jeanette
and
Mr. James Robert Simms
on Saturday, the eighth of May
at four o'clock
Parkway Country Club*

Or:

Mr. and Mrs. Dwight Charles Rich   (full name,
accept with pleasure the kind invitation no initials)
of
Doctor and Mrs. Arthur John McLendon (fullname
as it appears on the invitation)
for their daughter's wedding reception
on Saturday, the eighth of May
at four o'clock
Parkway Country Club*

THE FORMAL REGRET

It is not necessary to repeat the hour or the place in a regret.

Mr. and Mrs. Dwight Charles Rich
regret that they are unable to accept
Doctor and Mrs. Arthur John McLendon's (fullname
as it appears on the invitation)
kind invitation for
Saturday the eighth of May*

* All written by hand.

Or:

> *Mr. and Mrs. Dwight Charles Rich* (full name,
> *regret that they are unable to accept* no initials)
> *Doctor and Mrs. Arthur John McLendon's* (fullname
> as it appears on the invitation)
> *kind invitation*
> *for their daughter's wedding reception*
> *Saturday the eighth of May**

Regret stating reason:

> *Mr. and Mrs. Dwight Charles Rich*
> *regret exceedingly that* (or "regret that")
> *a previous engagement* (or "their absence
> *prevents their accepting* from the city")
> *Doctor and Mrs. Arthur John McLendon's* (name
> as it appears on the invitation)
> *kind invitation for*
> *Saturday the eighth of May**

Or if only one of the invited pair is able to accept:

> *Mrs. Dwight Charles Rich*
> *accepts with pleasure**
> *etc. . . .*

then add:

> *but regrets that Mr. Rich*
> *will be unable to attend**

FORMAL ACCEPTANCE OR REGRET BY TELEGRAM

Sometimes it is necessary to accept or regret a formal invitation by wire. If this is the case, the wording is the same as for any formal acceptance or regret.

ACCEPTANCE BY WIRE

Mr. and Mrs. Dwight Charles Rich accept with pleasure Dr. and Mrs. Arthur John McLendon's kind invitation for Saturday the eighth of May at four.

REGRET BY WIRE

Mr. and Mrs. Dwight Charles Rich regret that they are unable to accept Dr. and Mrs. Arthur John McLendon's kind invitation for Saturday May eighth.

* All written by hand.

ACCEPTANCE OR REGRET TO INFORMAL RECEPTION INVITATION

Invitations that are issued in the informal style are answered in the same informal way. The reply to an informal reception invitation is written in longhand on fine quality note paper or informal in blue-black or black ink.

The reply to an informal invitation should be sent as soon as possible after receiving the invitation.

There is no special wording for the informal answer. It reads very much the same way as the invitation.

Informals, or the fold-over card, with or without name (or names), engraved or printed, may be used for answering the informal invitation. If the inside of the informal is treated as note paper:

Dear Jeanette (no punctuation)
We are happy to accept your nice invitation for Saturday, the eighth, at four.
We are looking forward to being with you and appreciate so much your thinking of us.

Martha

Or:

Dear Jeanette (no punctuation)
We are so sorry we cannot accept your kind invitation for Saturday the eighth as we are leaving for the mountains on the fifth.
Thank you so much for thinking of us, and our love to the happy couple.

Martha

TELEPHONED ACCEPTANCE OR REGRET

An invitation issued by telephone is usually accepted or regretted at the time it is extended.

REPLIES WHEN THERE IS MORE THAN ONE BRIDE

If the invitation is for a reception when there are two brides and they are sisters, the usual acceptance or regret is sent, according to the formality of the invitation. If the brides are not sisters, the parents of both brides are sent acceptances or regrets conforming to the formality of the invitation.

RETURN ADDRESS

A return address may be handwritten, engraved, or embossed upon the back of the envelope.

Chapter 11. The Wedding Guest List

MAKING OUT THE GUEST LIST

The bride's mother or guardian, with the assistance of the bride and other members of her family, makes out the guest list.

The groom's mother and the groom send their lists with the addresses to the bride's mother as soon as possible.

WHEN THE LIST IS STARTED

The invitation list is started as soon as the engagement is announced (unless it is going to be a long engagement), especially if the wedding is to be very large.

THOSE INCLUDED IN THE GUEST LIST

The small wedding might include only relatives and close friends of the bride and groom.

The large wedding includes relatives and friends of the bride and groom and of their families, business associates of both fathers and of the groom, and families of the bridal attendants.

Invitations are sent to all members of the wedding party, to their parents, and to the minister and his wife.

SOURCES TO OBTAIN GUEST LIST

If the mother of the bride is making her own guest list without the assistance of a social secretary, there are a few suggested sources to aid her in remembering the names of guests to whom she will want to send invitations:

A guest list belonging to a friend who has recently had
a wedding.

Party list.

The telephone book, if your city is not too large.

Christmas card lists.

Church membership lists.

Business or social club lists.

Party lists that are published in the newspaper.

A pad and pencil kept handy at all times will prove
invaluable not only for jotting down the names of friends but
also for making a notation of any errands that must be done.

FORGETTING TO INVITE A FRIEND

The invitation list must be made out very carefully. It is
surprising how easy it is to leave out even a best friend. The
list should be gone over several times.

If, after the invitations have been mailed a few days, it is
discovered that a friend has been overlooked, an invitation
may still be sent.

If, on the other hand, the oversight is not discovered until
a few days before the ceremony, the friend should be called
and the oversight explained. She will understand. It is much
better to do this than to have her think the oversight was
intentional.

INVITATIONS TO OUT-OF-TOWN FRIENDS

Although it is quite correct to send wedding invitations to
out-of-town friends who will not be able to attend the ceremony, it is considerate not to include a reception invitation to
these friends (very close friends and relatives are the exception), as a reception invitation is interpreted by some as
requiring a gift. A reception invitation does not require a
gift if it is declined, but this is not always known. It is
thoughtful to send announcements to out-of-town friends who
will not be able to attend the wedding instead of reception
invitations or ceremony invitations that include a reception.

THE SOCIAL SECRETARY

Many times, when a wedding is to be large, a social secretary is employed to compile the invitation list and to address, seal, stamp, and mail the invitations.

Extra Invitations to the Groom's Family

It is thoughtful to send to the groom's family a few extra invitations which they might like to save as mementos of the occasion.

The Card File

Many times mothers try to compile a wedding list using an alphabetically lettered notebook. This method is not at all satisfactory as names cannot be written in a book in alphabetical order without making several copies. Time is wasted trying to locate a name and many times duplications are made.

An alphabetical card file is by far the most satisfactory method to use, as cards can be filed in their proper alphabetical position. It is practically impossible to make a duplication, and locating the name is facilitated.

The guest list might include one, two, or all of these categories:

1 ... Those who are to be sent ceremony invitations.
2 ... Those who are to be sent ceremony and reception invitations.
3 ... Those who are to be sent announcements.

1 ... If *all* guests are to be sent ceremony invitations or if *all* guests are to be sent ceremony and reception invitations.
   Materials needed for card file:

   a ... One set of alphabetical indexes.
   b ... One file box.
   c ... Plain white cards (3x5).

As acceptances or regrets for the reception arrive, that particular card is marked with "acc." for acceptance, or "reg." for regret. Thus a very quick tabulation can be made of how many guests to expect at the reception. As a general rule no one either accepts or regrets a ceremony invitation, so there is no reason to indicate this on these cards.

2 ... If *all* guests are invited to the ceremony and a fewer number to the reception or if *all* guests are invited to the reception and a fewer number to the ceremony.

Materials needed for card file:

a. Two sets of alphabetical indexes.
b. Two file boxes.
c. Plain white cards (3x5).
d. Colored cards, all the same color (3x5).

In the first box the white ceremony cards are filed.
In the second box the colored reception cards are filed.
As acceptances or regrets arrive, that person's card in the reception box is marked with "acc." for acceptance, or "reg." for regret. It is now very easy to make a quick tabulation of how many guests to expect at the reception.

As it is not necessary to reply to a ceremony invitation, there will be very few acceptances or regrets for these invitations.

3 . . . If announcements are being sent.

Announcement cards are filed in a separate box, using cards of another color, so that they may be addressed at the same time as the invitations but not mailed until after the ceremony. If announcements are being sent, a separate file should be kept for them.

HOW TO FILL OUT THE FILE CARDS

On each card is written the last name first, the title, then the complete given name and the correct and complete address the way it is to appear upon the invitation. Writing this all out correctly avoids questions later if someone is helping to address the invitations. Example:

Allen, Mr. and Mrs. Robert Howard

467 Grove Park Drive

Montego, California

The names of children (under 18) living at home are added:

Allen, Mr. and Mrs. Robert Howard

467 Grove Park Drive

Montego, California

Alice, John

Each guest name is written clearly upon the 3x5 card and the card is filed in alphabetical order in the file box for that particular category. The usual alphabetical procedure for filing should be followed; it is easier to locate a particular card if this is done. Before the addressing of invitations is started, the card file should be as complete as possible. This method is much more efficient than just jotting names down in a notebook with alphabetical headings, where many pages may have to be searched before a particular name is found.

If a second list is needed it is now very easy to make it from the alphabetical file.

GROWN CHILDREN

If the family includes children (over 18) living at home, they receive separate invitations. Their cards are made out and filed at the same time as their parents' cards. This is much quicker and easier than going back through all the cards later. The expense of sending separate invitations to grown children is slight. Since an invitation to a ceremony does not require a gift, a grown child, even though living in the home of his parents, should be sent a separate invitation.

Grown children may also be sent their own reception invitations. A grown child, living at home, may either send a separate wedding gift or his (or her) gift card (or name) may be enclosed in the wedding gift sent by his parents.

THE WORDS "AND FAMILY"

The use of the phrase "and family" is avoided in addressing invitations.

MAKING A SECOND LIST

If the bride is moving to another city after the wedding, it is a good plan for the bride's mother to have a record of all guests who were sent invitations. This can be done now very easily from the file. This second list is written in a notebook with alphabetical headings. This list may not seem important now, but later it will prove invaluable. The bride will need the card file to write her thank-you notes, which leaves the bride's mother with no record of the invited guests. There will be some gifts arriving after the wedding, and it is important that the mother of the bride have a record of her own. This second list will also be a great aid if there is a second daughter in the family, or it can be made available to a friend who is having a wedding. It can also be used for party lists later. A second list will be found quite worthwhile.

Chapter 12. Addressing Invitations and Announcements

HOW THEY ARE ADDRESSED

All invitations and announcements are addressed by hand. A blue-black or black ink is used.

TISSUES

Tissues that have been inserted in the invitations to keep the ink from smearing are left in the invitations.

ADDRESSING THE INVITATIONS

The bride, the bride's mother or guardian, any member of the bride's family, or a friend may help to address the invitations. Writing should be regular and legible; no one who does not write plainly should be asked to help.

SEALING

The inner envelope is left unsealed.
The outer envelope is sealed.

INSERTING THE INVITATION

Several leading engravers recommend that the inner envelope is inserted so that both envelopes face the same way.

101

A frequently used method is to place the unsealed envelope in the outer envelope so that it faces the flap.

Since there is no conformity regarding the proper method of insertion, the custom used locally might be the guide as to choice.

POSTAGE

All invitations and announcements are sent by first-class mail; a regulation five-cent stamp will suffice unless too many heavy enclosure cards are included.

DELIVERY OF ORDER

Orders of wedding invitations and announcements are delivered to the home of the bride unless specified otherwise.

INNER ENVELOPE—OUTER ENVELOPE

All wedding invitations have two envelopes.

The outer envelope is for the name and address of the person to whom it is being sent.

The inner envelope contains the invitation and any enclosure cards. On the inner envelope are written the title and the last name of the person to whom the invitation is being sent. No address is written upon the inner envelope.

ALREADY STUFFED

The inner envelope comes from the engravers already stuffed with the invitation and any enclosure cards.

OUTER ENVELOPE ADDRESSED BEFORE INVITATIONS ARE READY

The outer envelopes can be secured before the invitations are ready, making it possible to address them while waiting for the invitations to be engraved.

RETURN ADDRESS

Wedding invitations may be embossed on the back with the return address. It costs very little and is a courtesy to those being invited and to the postal authorities. Announcements carry no return address. "At Home" cards are used with announcements.

WHEN MAILED

Engraved invitations should be mailed four weeks before the ceremony.

Handwritten invitations are mailed two to three weeks before the ceremony.

Printed invitations are mailed four weeks before the ceremony.

Separate the in-town and out-of-town invitations as an aid to the post-office employees.

All invitations are mailed at the same time except those going overseas, which may be mailed a few days earlier.

Announcements are mailed as soon as possible after the ceremony.

THE NAME OF THE STATE NOT NECESSARY

Invitations or announcements mailed in the same city as that in which the wedding has or is to take place need not bear the name of the state.

Mr. and Mrs. Albert Lee Jones
245 Piedmont Place
Philadelphia

ABBREVIATIONS ALLOWABLE

All invited guests' names are written out in full, including the full middle name if it is known; if not, a middle initial may be used.

Abbreviations are not permitted except for "Mrs.," "Mr.," "Messrs.," "Dr.," "Jr.," and "Lt." when combined with Colonel, General, or Commander.

WRITE OUT IN FULL

The names of all cities, states, and streets.

The names of all invited guests.

All titles such as "Reverend," "Colonel," "Admiral," "Senator."

NOTE: Script denotes handwriting.

STREET NUMBERS

House numbers are written as such:

5679 Lane Drive

THE WORDS "AND FAMILY"

Do not use the phrase "and family."

SYMBOLS

Do not use the symbol "&," such as:

· *Mr. & Mrs. Allen*

The correct form is:

Mr. and Mrs. Allen

TEENAGE OR GROWN CHILDREN'S CEREMONY INVITATIONS

Since there is no gift obligation attached to a *ceremony* invitation, nor is an answer necessary, the teenage or grown children may be sent their own ceremony invitations; the extra expense for a few invitations will be slight.

TEENAGE OR GROWN CHILDREN'S RECEPTION INVITATIONS

If teenage or grown children are sent their own *reception* invitations, they are expected to reply. If the invitations are accepted, their names may be included on the enclosed gift card sent by their parents. They send a separate gift, however, if their parents have not been invited.

ADDRESSING FORM

Outer envelope:

Mr. and Mrs. Walter Simpson Allen
467 Grove Park Drive
Davenport
Iowa

Inner envelope:

Mr. and Mrs. Allen

NOTE: Script denotes handwriting.

Small Children

If the family includes *small children* and they are to be invited, their names are written under the names of their parents on the INNER envelope only.

Outer envelope:

> *Mr. and Mrs. Walter Simpson Allen*
> *467 Grove Park Drive*
> *Davenport*
> *Iowa*

Inner envelope:

> *Mr. and Mrs. Allen*
> *Jean, Jane and John*

IF THE SMALL CHILDREN ARE TO BE SENT THEIR OWN INVITATIONS

Outer envelope:

> *The Misses Allen*
> *The Messrs. Allen*
> *467 Grove Park Drive*
> *etc.*

Inner envelope:

> *Jean, Jane, Charles and John Allen*

Teenage Children

A teenage child may be sent a separate invitation, but more often the child is invited by writing her (or his) name (or names) upon the INNER envelope of the invitation issued to the parents.

Outer envelope:

> *Mr. and Mrs. Walter Simpson Allen*
> *467 Grove Park Drive*
> *etc.*

Inner envelope:

> *Mr. and Mrs. Allen*
> *Miss Nancy Allen*
> *Kendrick Allen*

NOTE: Script denotes handwriting.

If a teenage child is sent an individual invitation, the form is the same as for a grown child except that "Master" is used for a boy under twelve. His given name is used from twelve to eighteen; after eighteen he is "Mr."

GROWN CHILDREN

Grown sons or daughters (over 18) living with their parents or at some other address should receive their own invitations.

GROWN DAUGHTER

Outer envelope:

Miss Jane Allen
467 Grove Park Drive
etc.

Inner envelope:

Miss Allen

GROWN SON

Outer envelope:

Mr. John Allen
467 Grove Park Drive
etc.

Inner envelope:

Mr. Allen

TWO OR MORE GROWN DAUGHTERS

Two or more grown daughters may receive one invitation.

Outer envelope:

Misses Jane and Jean Allen   (or The Misses
467 Grove Park Drive Jane and Jean Allen)
etc.

Inner envelope:

Misses Allen   (or The Misses Allen)

NOTE: Script denotes handwriting.

TWO OR MORE GROWN SONS

Two or more grown sons may receive one invitation.

Outer envelope:

> *Messrs. John and James Allen*
> *467 Grove Park Drive*
> *etc.*

Inner envelope:

> *Messrs. Allen* (or The Messrs. Allen)

ADULT WOMEN AT THE SAME ADDRESS

Adult women living at the same address receive separate invitations.

Adult daughter or daughters, mother or other female adult relative, companion, housekeeper, nurse, or any other adult woman living in the same household of a family being invited to a wedding or reception receives her own invitation.

ADULT MEN AT THE SAME ADDRESS

Adult men living at the same address receive separate invitations.

Adult son or sons, father or other male relative, companion, secretary, nurse, or any other adult male living in the same household of a family invited must receive a separate invitation.

WIDOW'S TITLE

A widow's title is the same as though her husband were still alive.

DIVORCEE'S TITLE

The divorcee's title is a combination of her married and maiden surnames: Mrs. Brown Jones, Brown being her name before she was married.

IF A HUSBAND OR A WIFE IS UNKNOWN TO SENDER

Invitations are addressed to a husband and wife even if the sender knows only one of the couple.

NOTE: Script denotes handwriting.

MILITARY TITLES FOR ADDRESSING

When addressing invitations or announcements to members of the armed forces, it is customary to include their titles.

Outer envelope:

Captain Arthur Pope Williams
address

Inner envelope:

Captain Williams

Or:

Outer envelope:

Captain and Mrs. Arthur Pope Williams
address

Inner envelope:

Captain and Mrs. Williams

GOVERNMENT OFFICIALS

THE PRESIDENT OF THE UNITED STATES

The President and Mrs. Smith
The White House
Washington, D. C.

THE VICE-PRESIDENT OF THE UNITED STATES

The Vice-President and Mrs. Smith
Home Address
Washington, D. C.

THE CHIEF JUSTICE OF THE SUPREME COURT

The Chief Justice and Mrs. Smith
Home Address

ASSOCIATE JUSTICE

Mr. Justice and Mrs. Smith
Home Address

CABINET OFFICER

The Secretary of Labor and Mrs. Smith
Home Address

NOTE: Script denotes handwriting.

UNDER SECRETARY

The Under Secretary of State and Mrs. Smith
Home Address

ASSISTANT SECRETARY

The Honorable and Mrs. Arthur Smith
Home Address

AMERICAN AMBASSADOR

His Excellency, The American Ambassador and Mrs. Smith
American Embassy

AMERICAN MINISTER

The American Minister and Mrs. Smith
American Legation

SENATOR

The Honorable and Mrs. Arthur Smith
Home Address

REPRESENTATIVE

The Honorable and Mrs. Arthur Smith

GOVERNOR

His Excellency, the Governor of Iowa and Mrs. Smith
Executive Mansion
Des Moines, Iowa

MAYOR

The Honorable and Mrs. Arthur Smith
Home Address

JUDGE

The Honorable and Mrs. Arthur Smith
Home Address

NOTE: Script denotes handwriting.

PROTESTANT CLERGY

EPISCOPAL BISHOP

The Right Reverend and Mrs. Smith
Home Address

ARCHDEACON

The Archdeacon of Louisville and Mrs. Smith
Home Address

DEAN

The Very Reverend and Mrs. Arthur Smith
Home Address

CANON

The Reverend and Mrs. Arthur Smith
Home Address

METHODIST BISHOP

The Very Reverend and Mrs. Arthur Smith
Home Address

PROTESTANT CLERGYMAN

The Reverend and Mrs. Arthur Smith
Home Address

ROMAN CATHOLIC

THE POPE

His Holiness, The Pope
Vatican City
Italy

CARDINAL

His Eminence
Arthur Cardinal Smith
Denver, Colorado

NOTE: Script denotes handwriting.

ARCHBISHOP

The Most Reverend Arthur Smith
Archbishop of Denver
Denver, Colorado

BISHOP

The Most Reverend Arthur Smith
Bishop of Denver
Denver, Colorado

MONSIGNOR

The Right Reverend Arthur Smith
Church Address

PRIEST

The Reverend Arthur Smith (and initials of
Church Address   religious order)

MOTHER SUPERIOR

The Reverend Mother Superior (and initials of
Church Address   her order)

SISTER

Sister Mary Smith
Address

BROTHER

The Reverend Brother Arthur Smith
Address

HEBREW

RABBI WITH SCHOLASTIC DEGREE

Rabbi (or Dr.) and Mrs. Arthur Smith
Home Address

RABBI WITHOUT SCHOLASTIC DEGREE

Rabbi and Mrs. Arthur Smith
Home Address

NOTE: Script denotes handwriting.

OTHER

MEN
Mr. Arthur Smith

AN UNMARRIED WOMAN
Miss Mary Smith

A MARRIED WOMAN
Mrs. Arthur Smith

A DIVORCED WOMAN
Mrs. Jones Smith   (Jones being her maiden name)

A WIDOW
Mrs. Arthur Smith

CHILDREN
Female: "Miss" at any age.

Male: "Master": for boys under twelve. No title between twelve and eighteen. "Mr." after eighteen.

NOTE: Script denotes handwriting.

Chapter 13. Parties

Too Many Parties

After the engagement has been announced, friends will be eager to entertain for the bride and for the bride and groom. Parties are fun, and they are meant to be just that. Too many crowded into too short a period of time, or too many late parties, result in the entire wedding party and both families being completely exhausted before the actual wedding day arrives, as most party lists include all members of the wedding party and many would include relatives of both families. If it is at all possible, wedding festivities should be limited to a period of a week or ten days before the ceremony. Too many late parties should not be scheduled, especially a few days before the ceremony.

Showers may be included, but here again is a word of warning. Too many showers become very expensive for the bride's attendants, as they are all included in the guest lists (unless it is a special group party) and each shower calls for another gift. Members of the bride's and groom's immediate family do not give showers.

When friends call expressing a desire to entertain for the bridal pair, preference should be given to the first friend expressing such a desire. The gracious offer of one friend should not be refused and then a later offer from another friend accepted unless there is some very good reason for so doing and the circumstances are understood.

If a party calendar is filled when a friend offers to entertain, it should be explained that there is no more time available for parties. Friends will understand and perhaps they can give a party later.

MAKING OUT THE GUEST LIST

The bride (or the bride and her mother) makes out the guest list for the engagement announcement party, even though someone other than the bride's parents is giving the party.

A hostess makes out the guest list for a bridal party IF the party is being given to introduce the bride. If the party is not being given to introduce the bride, it is the custom for the hostess to ask the bride or the bride and her mother to furnish the guest list.

A hostess who has expressed her desire to entertain designates a date, a time, and the number of guests that can be accommodated. If the guest list is being furnished by the bride, under no circumstances does she include more names than the specified number. The bride should include the address and telephone number of each guest and then deliver or mail the list *immediately* to her hostess. A hostess should never have to call a second time for a guest list.

THE GUESTS

The guest list for special parties is given later in this chapter.

Traditionally, certain people are invited to all pre-wedding parties.

Parties for the bride include the bride, her attendants, mothers of the flower girl and/or ring bearer, sisters and sisters-in-law, and feminine members of the bride's and groom's families. Larger parties for the bride should also include the bride's friends, friends of the bride's and groom's mothers, relatives, out-of-town relatives, and friends.

Parties for the groom would include the groom, his attendants, male relatives, and friends.

Parties for the bride and groom include the bride and groom, their attendants and their wives or husbands, and any other couples the bride and groom wish to invite.

SOME SUGGESTED PARTIES

Breakfasts, luncheons, or dinners, either seated or buffet. Coffee, coke parties, or afternoon teas. After dinner coffees or dessert parties. Bridge or canasta parties, either luncheons, dessert, or after dinner. Cocktail parties. Outdoor parties such as barbecues, boating, skiing, skating, or swimming parties. A mother-daughter party. A tea given at the bride's home so friends may see the wedding presents. An out-of-town guest party. The engagement announcement party. The bridesmaids' party. The rehearsal dinner. The bachelor dinner or party.

FORMAL LUNCHEON (TO HONOR A GUEST)

Mrs. David Wise Melton
requests the honour of your company
at luncheon in honour of
Miss Sylvia Jane Morris
on Friday, the first of June
at one o'clock
Fifty-five Terrace Road
Davenport

Please Reply

AFTERNOON TEA

Mrs. David Wise Melton
Mrs. Robert Cyrus Stuart
At Home
Wednesday afternoon, the third of May
from four until six o'clock
2456 Arlington Boulevard
Raleigh

SOME SUGGESTED SHOWERS

Linen, lingerie, kitchen, pantry, bar, stocking, closet, garden, apron, toilet article, dish towel, towel, bathroom, sewing, gadget, fix-it-yourself, miscellaneous.

SPECIAL PARTIES

THE ENGAGEMENT ANNOUNCEMENT PARTY

Having an engagement announcement party is completely a matter of choice; but if there is one, it is usually given by the bride's parents or a relative, and in some cases by close friends of the bride's family.

The engagement announcement party may be given at home, or at a club, hotel, or restaurant.

Sometimes the bride's home is too small to accommodate the number of guests who are to be invited and a close friend offers her larger home for the occasion. In this case the bride's parents pay all expenses of the party, including food, liquid refreshment, flowers used, and the salaries of any domestic help or professional services needed. The bride's mother and father are the host and hostess for the occasion and they greet the guests, make out the guest list, etc.

The size or type of the engagement party is a matter of choice. It may be a formal seated affair or the simplest morning coffee. A very small party includes the bride and groom and members of both families. A larger party includes the bride and groom, their attendants and their wives or husbands, members of both families, and friends.

The engagement party may be as formal or as informal as the host and hostess desire it to be. If the party is very formal, engraved invitations are issued by the host and hostess for the occasion. If engraved invitations are issued, it is practically a promise that a large formal wedding will follow. If the wedding is to be less formal, it is more in keeping for the bride's mother to issue handwritten invitations. See page 60. Printed or illustrated invitations are not appropriate for this occasion.

It is not accepted as being in good taste for the groom's parents to give the engagement announcement party. They may entertain for the engaged couple after the engagement has been officially announced.

If a friend or relative is giving the engagement announcement party, the guest list is furnished by the bride or the bride and her mother. The hostess should give the bride an approximate number of guests to invite, and the bride (or the bride and her mother) makes out the list, keeping within this number. The list is then either taken or mailed immediately to the hostess, complete with addresses and telephone numbers.

In a large or sophisticated community or city, the engagement is often announced in the newspaper before the engagement announcement party. At such a party, after the guests have assembled, the father of the bride proposes a toast to his daughter and her fiance; the groom-to-be then answers with a toast to the bride and her family; other toasts follow.

In less formal communities the engagement is often made known at an engagement announcement party before the announcement is published in the newspaper. As each guest arrives, or after they have assembled, clever favors announce the happy event or the bride's father may propose a toast to the affianced couple. If favors are used to announce the engagement, they contain the first names of the bride and groom and are often tiny wedding bells, wedding rings, miniature dolls, etc. If the party is seated, amusing place cards may tell the news, or a wedding cake may be used for the table center piece, or sometimes ice-cream molds or individual wedding cakes tell of the wedding that is to come. If the announcement is to be a surprise, it should be made certain that the news does not come out in the newspaper before the surprise announcement party.

The engagement ring is not worn until after the engagement has been officially announced, but it may be worn at the announcement party.

THE BRIDESMAIDS' PARTY

This party may be given by one or more of several people: either the bride, her mother, the groom's mother, a female relative, one or more of the bridal attendants, or one or more close friends or relatives of either the bride or the groom.

A large bridesmaids' party includes the bride, her attendants, her hostess, both mothers, mothers of the flower girl and ring bearer, sisters and sisters-in-law of the bride and groom, and any female relative or friend the bride wishes to invite. A smaller party includes the bride, her attendants, the two mothers, and the hostess.

The bride furnishes her hostess with the list of guests' names, complete with addresses and telephone numbers.

The bridesmaids' party is usually a luncheon, but it may be a party of any type that would be enjoyed by a group of young ladies. It may be held at home or in a club, restaurant, hotel, or tearoom.

A very old but still enjoyable tradition is the serving of a cake in which has been baked:

A dime .... for riches
A ring .... for first to be married
A thimble .... the old maid
Wishbone .... luckiest
Boat .... for travel
Boy doll .... romance
Girl doll .... a rival
Miniature cow or horse... live in the country

At the bridesmaids' party the bride presents her gifts to her attendants, thus the reason for not usually inviting anyone other than the attendants and very close relatives. A gift for the flower girl, if there is one, is given to her mother.

After the bridesmaids' party the guests drop by the bride's home to view the wedding presents.

If the hostess is someone other than the bride or her mother, she usually presents the bride with a small gift as a memento of the occasion.

The bridesmaids' party is held a few days before the ceremony.

THE REHEARSAL PARTY

This party is given before or after the wedding rehearsal. It may be given by the bride's parents, the groom's parents, close relatives, or friends. Many times the groom's parents are the host and hostess, especially if they live in the same city as the bride and her family. If the groom's parents live in another city, arrangements can be made for this party by contacting a club or hotel in the bride's city, the bride's mother helping with these arrangements.

All members of the wedding party are invited as well as members of both immediate families. Sometimes included are the minister and his wife, the organist and soloist and their wives or husbands, and husbands and wives of attendants. Out-of-town relatives and friends should be included.

The guest list is furnished by the bride. If this party is to be small and/or informal, invitations are issued verbally. If it is to be large, the hostess may write or telephone each guest. If the rehearsal party is to be formal, engraved invitations are issued.

Placecards are used at a seated dinner, the bride and groom sitting at the head of the table, the groom's mother seated on the right of the bride's father, and the bride's mother seated on the right of the groom's father. See "Bride's and Parents' Table" (p. 242) for seating arrangement.

Toasts may be proposed, the host proposing the first one to the bride and the groom.

Attendants' gifts are given at this party if there has been no bachelor or bridesmaids' party, where gifts are usually presented.

A word of warning—if this party is given the night before the ceremony the party should not be prolonged as the next day is a busy one.

The formal invitation for the rehearsal dinner:

> *Mr. and Mrs. James Arthur Barry*
> *request the pleasure of your company*
> *at dinner*
> *on Saturday, the first of May*
> *at seven o'clock*
> *Lakewood Country Club*

R.S.V.P.
7810 Arbor Road

or:

> *Mr. and Mrs. Harry Thomas Sanders*
> *request the pleasure of the company of*
> (guest's name handwritten in)
> *at dinner*
> *on Saturday, the fourth of May*
> *at eight o'clock*
> *Country Club of Charleston*
> *Charleston*

Please reply to
64 Brentwood Street

or:

> *In honour of*   (or in honor of)
> *Miss Sylvia Ann Jones*
> *and*
> *Mr. Henry Arthur Bishop*
> *Doctor and Mrs. Emory Charles Bishop*
> *request the pleasure of your company*
> *at dinner*
> *Wednesday evening, the tenth of May*
> *at eight o'clock*
> *The Driving Club*
> *Seattle*

Please reply to
9310 Sylvan Road

See "Bride's and Parents' Table" (p. 242) for formal seating arrangement.

THE BACHELOR PARTY

This party is nearly always given by the groom, but it may be given by the best man or one or more of the groom's attendants.

On this occasion the groom presents his gifts to his attendants. (Suggestions are given in this chapter.)

The bachelor party is usually a gay stag affair, and it may be one where a complete dinner is served with wine or mixed drinks, or it may take the form of a cocktail party with mixed drinks and canapés.

The bachelor party may be held at home or in a private room at a club, hotel, or restaurant.

Toward the end of the festivities, the traditional toast is proposed by the groom "to the bride," and all the guests rise and respond to the toast. Although it used to be the custom to break the glasses after this toast, either by throwing them into the fireplace or some other suitable place or by breaking the stems, custom no longer demands this gesture and the glasses are usually drained and replaced upon the table.

The bachelor party is held a few days before the ceremony, and the guest list includes the male members of the wedding party and any other male relatives or friends the host and the groom wish to include.

THE OUT-OF-TOWN GUEST PARTY

One of the very nicest parties is the one given for the out-of-town guests. This party is given the day of the wedding and may be a breakfast if the ceremony is in the middle of the morning or at noon, a luncheon if the ceremony is in the middle of the afternoon, or an early buffet supper if the ceremony is in the evening.

This party is always informal and may or may not include the members of the bridal party. Invitations are issued by word of mouth and include all out-of-town guests, relatives, and any other friends the hostess and the bride's mother wish to include.

As this party is a courtesy to the bride's mother, it is usually given by one (or more) of her closest friends or a relative. Food is served buffet style and alcoholic beverages are not served, since this party is given shortly before the ceremony.

This party eliminates all the extra hustle and bustle at the bride's home on the day of the ceremony as well as getting all of the out-of-town relatives and friends together for a friendly chat.

THANK-YOU LETTERS TO A HOSTESS

Every hostess is written a thank-you note for her party. The bride writes each hostess as soon as possible after the party. Many times a hostess will give the bride a small personal gift as a memento of the party; if this is done, a thank-you for this is included in the letter. If a party has been given by a couple, the thank-you note is addressed to the hostess, but the host is mentioned in the body of the letter. If more than one hostess entertained at the same party, a thank-you note is written to each.

When a bride writes her hostess a thank-you letter for giving a shower, she also thanks the hostess for the shower gift. A verbal thank-you at the time she opens the gifts is all that is necessary to the other invited guests. If a friend who is unable to come sends a shower gift, the bride writes her a thank-you note.

USING INFORMALS FOR PARTY INVITATIONS

If handwritten informal invitations to a party are to be issued, the informal or fold-over card may be used, with name or names printed or engraved. If an invitation is being issued by a hostess, she uses her own informal, printed or engraved with her name only. If an invitation is being issued by a host and hostess, the informal carries both their names.

If visiting cards are being used, the same rules as above apply.

Invitation on informal or visiting card:

Cocktails Friday
Mr. and Mrs. Raymond Charles Adams
May 20th, 8-10

25 Alden Way

Monday, April 10, 5:00
Mrs. Raymond Charles Adams

R.S.V.P.   *25 Alden Way*

NOTE: Script denotes handwriting.

Chapter 14. Wedding Gifts

SELECTING SILVER, CRYSTAL, AND CHINA PATTERNS

It has long been the accepted custom for the bride and groom to select their own patterns of silver, crystal, and china, and this is a very sensible custom. It not only enables the bride and groom to have the patterns of their choice, but it also assists the donors to choose a gift that they know will please and be appropriate.

These patterns are selected at the store or stores most likely to be patronized by most of the bride's and groom's friends, either a bridal gift consultant shop, a fine jewelry store, a gift shop, specialty shop, or some department stores. These stores keep a registered account of all gift selections and the number of articles sold in each pattern so that few duplications are made.

Occasionally a selection of linens is also made. Here again these are selected from a store or stores most likely to be patronized by the majority of the invited guests.

If the wedding is to be large, a second pattern of silver or china is often chosen, usually less expensive china and plated silver. This gives friends a wider variety in price range.

Choosing open-stock china and crystal makes replacement easier.

No matter how small the wedding is to be, pattern selections should be made. Even a few pieces of silver, china, or crystal will provide a start and can be added to later.

Engagement Presents

No one is obligated to send an engagement present. If one is sent, however, it is acknowledged with a thank-you note unless it is from the bride's parents or the groom-to-be.

All congratulatory cards, letters, and telegrams should also receive an acknowledgment.

Bridal Gift Consultant Shops

If there is a bridal gift consultant shop in the community a bride and her mother are most fortunate. These modern shops have a trained staff to assist the bride and her mother with all wedding gift problems and with any questions that might arise about the invitations. They will also furnish some of the articles to help with the gift display and the reception.

They will help with the selection of invitations, announcements, and enclosure cards, and give advice as to the wording for any special case. If silver, china, or crystal patterns are selected at their shops, they keep a registered record of the selections and see that no duplications are sold.

Some of these shops will make suggestions for the arranging of gifts, and some will send a member of their staff to the home of the bride to assist with the arranging. Many will supply plate and tray racks to hold large platters or plates.

For the reception these shops may furnish cups, both coffee and punch, punch bowls and ladles, tablecloths, extra plates, a silver coffee service, extra tables and chairs, as well as many other articles needed for the reception.

These shops are of tremendous help to the bride and her mother during a wedding; and if the bride has selected her wedding gift patterns at one of them, their services are free. Their information on weddings is accurate.

Monogrammed Linens

Linens are monogrammed with the bride's future initials: when Mary Howard marries John Pope, the initials would be M. H. P. If one initial is used, it would be the initial of the groom's surname, in this case "P".

Engraved Silver

Initials may be engraved in many ways; a good jeweler will suggest the one best suited to a particular silver pattern.

Mary Howard marries John Pope:

If a single letter is being used, it may be the first letter of the groom's surname (P). The bride may prefer to use the first letter of her maiden surname (H).

If three letters are being used, it may be the first initial of the bride's first name, her maiden surname, and her married surname (M. H. P.); or it may be the initial of both the bride's and groom's first names centered below or above the initial of their surname   M J   P
(P),   (M J).

Silver may also be engraved with either the bride's family crest or the groom's.

Gifts the Bride and Groom Give

GIFTS TO EACH OTHER

The groom's gift to his bride is often a piece of jewelry which she can wear with her wedding dress; if finances must be watched, a small gift with a great deal of sentiment is much better than trying to buy a very expensive gift.

The bride's gift to the groom is also often a small piece of jewelry; if finances must be watched, a small sentimental gift of any kind is more appropriate than a very expensive gift.

GIFTS TO THE WEDDING ATTENDANTS

A list of suggestions is given later in this chapter.

The bride traditionally presents her gift to her attendants at the bridesmaids' party. If there is no such party, she may present them any time before the ceremony. Gifts to the bride's attendants are usually alike, but the honor attendant's gift may vary in style and design.

Gifts to the groom's attendants are traditionally presented at the bachelor party or dinner; if there is no such party, they are either given at the rehearsal party or a few days before the ceremony.

Gifts to the ushers are all alike, but the best man's gift may vary in style and design.

If the wedding is to be formal, the groom also gives the ushers and the best man their ties and gloves to be worn at the ceremony.

A small gift should be given to the flower girl and the ring bearer, the bride buying the flower girl's gift, the groom buying the ring bearer's gift.

GIFT TO A HIGH-RANKING OFFICIAL WHO PERFORMS
THE CEREMONY

If a high-ranking official such as mayor, governor, or Supreme Court judge has performed the ceremony as a special favor to either of the families, he is not given a fee. A gift is sent to him later by the bride and groom, along with a note of thanks.

GIFT SUGGESTIONS FOR THE BRIDE'S ATTENDANTS

Silver picture frames, a picture of the bridal party sent later to use in the frame.

Silver spoons (nut, jam, or demi-tasse) engraved with both first names of the bride and groom.

Pearls or some piece of jewelry to be worn at the ceremony.

Charm bracelet with two hearts, one heart engraved with the bride's name and one with the groom's name.

Cigarette boxes, silver pencils or pens, gold or silver thimbles, dainty pill boxes, cigarette lighters, vanity cases, letter openers, charms for bracelets, evening purses, Saint Christopher medals, jeweled lipsticks, jeweled clocks, dainty pin cushion, travel clocks, perfume, jewelry cases. The bridal gift consultant shop can help with other suggestions.

Honor attendants' gifts are usually the same as the bridesmaids' but may vary in size or design.

GIFT SUGGESTIONS FOR THE GROOM'S ATTENDANTS

Leather or silver desk accessories, cigarette boxes, travel clocks. Jewelry such as studs, tie clasps, cuff links, belt buckles. Jewelry cases, usually leather with initial. Leather picture frame with or without picture of the wedding party. Leather, zippered, toilet article case. Cigarette lighter, usually engraved with the attendant's initial. Flasks, leather or silver. Billfold, leather with or without initial. Money clip. Pen and pencil set. Leather photograph folder. Silver jigger, with or without initial. Silver or gold bottle opener, with or without initial.

At a formal wedding the groom also gives his attendants their gloves and ties worn at the ceremony.

SPECIAL GIFTS

GIFTS FROM THE PARENTS

It is customary for the bride's parents and the groom's parents to give the bride and groom the loveliest wedding present that they are able to afford. Silver seems to be the most popular choice because of its lasting quality and beauty, but many times the bride and groom prefer something else and the choice is left up to them.

GIFTS FROM THE ATTENDANTS

Each attendant sends a wedding present, no matter how small, to the bride and groom.

As a general rule, the bride's attendants are close family friends or relatives and their gift card is included in the gift from their family to the bride and groom. If this is not the case, they send individual presents.

Some lumber supply stores will loan the saw-horses to a prospective bride for a few weeks. This is a service that many builder-supply stores are happy to provide; if it is offered, your bridal consultant store will know about it. One saw-horse is needed at each end of an eight-foot table, or three saw-horses will take care of the long table two feet wide by sixteen feet long. These saw-horses are not expensive if they must be purchased, and they can be ordered over the telephone and delivered to the bride's home.

Many times tables can be rented from a rental service or from women's clubs, etc. The bridal gift consultant shop will know from whom they may be rented or a rental service might be listed in the yellow pages of the telephone directory.

MOVING FURNITURE TO MAKE ROOM FOR THE GIFT DISPLAY

Some of the larger pieces of furniture will probably have to be moved to make room for the gift display. If all gifts can be displayed in one room, the task of arranging them is made much easier; and it is simpler to check the number of articles in each particular group.

ARRANGING GIFTS

Gifts should be arranged artistically, with particular types together, such as all silver, all china, etc. Tables look better this way, and the packing of gifts later is made easier. Bridal gift consultant shops sometimes assist with the arranging of gifts. Inquiry about this service should be made if the wedding gifts are being purchased at one of these shops. If this service is furnished, it is free.

Many times the ushers send a combined gift, to which each usher has contributed his part. If this is not done, each usher sends an individual gift.

DISPLAYING WEDDING GIFTS

DISPLAY TABLES

Tables will be needed on which to display the wedding gifts, even if the wedding is quite small.

In some cities these tables are furnished by the bridal gift consultant stores; or if they do not furnish them, they can give information as to where they might be obtained.

A friend who has recently had a wedding may be glad to loan her tables, or she may be able to give advice as to where they can be obtained.

Card tables can be used for displaying linens and unbreakable gifts. They are certainly not practical to use for displaying breakable articles.

If tables must be bought, they are not too expensive nor are they too difficult to assemble. The tops of the tables can be made from ¾ inch plywood, with wooden saw-horses used for the legs. Plywood comes in sheets four feet by eight feet. In order to make a table two feet wide by eight feet long, one sheet of plywood is cut in half on the four-foot side. Or two tables two feet wide by eight feet long can be made from one sheet of plywood. The plywood can be ordered from the lumber or millwork company over the telephone, cut and delivered to the bride's home.

DECORATING THE GIFT DISPLAY TABLES

The display tables should be covered with white or very pale colored cloth. Sheets or white tablecloths are usually used for this. This cloth should reach the floor on the front of the tables. Lace tablecloths may be placed over the white cloth to give a prettier effect, or it may be left plain. Rayon satin is often used to cover the tables and is very effective and reasonable in price. Discarded sheer curtains are sometimes used if they are still in good condition.

After the tables are covered, a little decoration may be added. White satin ribbon tied with tiny white flowers and pinned to the front of the tables in a drape effect is very attractive. Some beautiful bows will come tied to the wedding gifts; these might be pinned to the front of the table drape.

CHECKS

Checks are not displayed; instead, the amount of the check is written on a small white card and the card is displayed; the name of the donor is not written on the card. Such as: Check . . . $25

BOXES TO BE SAVED

Small boxes in which the wedding presents arrive may be stored for the time being under the display table.

GIFT CARDS

Save all gift cards that accompany the wedding gifts. Cards may be displayed on the gifts, but more often they are not. See the section, "Recording Gifts," for proper handling of gift cards.

INSTRUCTION PAMPHLETS

Save all instruction sheets and warranty cards accompanying electrical appliances or other gifts.

FELT AND PLASTIC SILVER COVERS

Save all felt or plastic silver covers. These may be used later as a protection against tarnish.

DISPLAY RACKS

Display racks for large trays or platters can usually be obtained at the store where most of the wedding gifts are bought; a gift consultant store will usually loan these. They must be returned after the wedding.

Moving to Another City

If the bride and groom are moving to another city after the honeymoon, it is a good plan to have any large cartons or boxes in which card tables, television tables, lamps, blankets, luggage racks, or luggage, etc., were originally packed. They will fit much better into these boxes than any other container a packer might use.

Insurance Policy

A floating policy may be placed on the wedding gifts, and it is an excellent plan to do this, especially if the gifts are many in number and/or they are to be shipped later. These policies usually give coverage for a three-month period and also take care of any damage in shipping. An insurance company is contacted about this.

A Professional Guard for the Wedding Presents

If the wedding gifts are numerous and the house will be empty during the wedding and reception, it is advisable to employ a professional guard during this time. The police department or a private bureau may be contacted here.

If Gifts Arrive Broken

If a gift arrives broken and it has been purchased locally, the store should be called immediately. Wedding gifts are covered by insurance and the broken article will be replaced.

If a gift arrives broken from an out-of-town store, wrapped and shipped by them, the store should be written immediately and inquiry made regarding instructions as to how the gift will be replaced.

If a gift arrives broken from an out-of-town friend, wrapped and shipped by that friend but insured, the friend should be written explaining the breakage. The insurance will cover the broken article.

If a gift arrives from an out-of-town friend, wrapped and shipped by her, but not insured, it is best to write a thank-you note for the gift as though it had arrived in perfect condition. The reason for this is obvious; if the friend were told that her gift had arrived broken, she would feel obligated to send another gift; and since the gift carried no insurance, she would be spending twice as much as she originally planned to invest.

Gift Card Missing or Not Legible

If a gift card is missing or the gift card is not legible, the store from which the gift was purchased should be notified immediately. A record is kept at the store and they will supply the donor's name.

EXCHANGING GIFTS

Gifts may be exchanged if a number of the identical article has been received. This must be carefully done to avoid hurting anyone's feelings. Rather than risk hurting a good friend's feelings, it is better to keep the gift even though at the time it seems unlikely that it will ever be used. Only if the gift can be exchanged without the donor having any knowledge of it should this be done.

RETURNING GIFTS WHEN THE ENGAGEMENT IS BROKEN

If an engagement is permanently broken, ALL wedding gifts MUST be returned.

Each gift is accompanied by a note from either the bride or the bride's mother saying that the wedding plans have been terminated and thanking them for their kindness in sending the gift. No explanation of why the wedding plans were changed is necessary.

RETURNING GIFTS WHEN THE MARRIAGE IS BROKEN

Even if the marriage lasts only a few days or weeks, the wedding gifts are not returned unless they have been unopened and unused. If they are returned, they are accompanied by a thank-you note. No explanation of why the marriage was terminated is necessary. If a marriage is broken, wedding gifts are divided equally, between the husband and wife.

THE CONSIDERATE BRIDE

With all the excitement of the gifts arriving and the hustle and bustle of the wedding, it is very easy to forget that the groom's family want to and should share in this happy time. The parents of the groom are placed in an awkward situation when they are unaware of the gifts sent by their friends. The gracious bride or her mother will identify these gifts and not make it necessary for the groom's family to seek the information in devious ways. Consideration in this matter creates a warm feeling between the two families; carelessness, on the other hand, causes embarrassment to the groom's family with resultant resentment. It is a wise and thoughtful bride who will take the time to call her future in-laws and invite them over every few days to view the wedding gifts and to share in any new development of the wedding plans. If the groom's family lives in another city, the bride should write them an occasional note telling of the gifts received, especially those received from friends of the groom's family. This takes only a few minutes and is well worth the time spent.

RECORDING GIFTS

HOW THEY ARE RECORDED

Recording gifts is very simple if ALL gifts are properly recorded in the gift book as soon as they are opened.

It is not a good plan to have too many people opening gifts at one time. This is confusing and mistakes are more easily made.

Purchase of the correct size gift book to suit the wedding should be made. Gift books can be obtained to keep a record of from fifty to one thousand gifts. These books are sold at the bridal gift consultant shop, gift shops, specialty shops, stationery and department stores.

As each present arrives and is opened, the sender's name and address, a description of the gift, the shop where it was purchased, and the date it is received are recorded in the gift book. The date on which the thank-you note is written is also recorded. Such as:

No. Donor	Address	Descr. of gift	Bought from	Date rec'd.	Thank you
1. Mr. and Mrs. James Ivey	7 Cove Dr.	Pair of silver candlesticks	Home and Hobby	Jan. 2	Jan. 7
2. Mr. and Mrs. Fred Ware	18 Arden Dr.	Blue ash tray	Jane's Jewelry	Jan. 3	Jan. 7
3. ———					
4. ———					

All gift cards that come with the wedding presents must be saved; THIS IS IMPORTANT. A special box to hold these cards should be provided. As soon as the gift is opened, the bride should write, on the back of each card, what the gift is, the store where it was purchased, and the number that corresponds to that in the bridal gift book. This gives a second check on all wedding gifts.

A THIRD RECORD OF GIFTS[*]

Many times a third record is needed of wedding gifts, especially if the bride is moving to another city or when the wedding gifts are so numerous that a mistake could easily be made.

In this case the alphabetical card file that was used for the wedding guest list is used.

As a present arrives and is opened, it is recorded in the bridal gift book, a description of the gift is written upon the back of each enclosed gift card, and the gift is recorded on that particular person's card in the alphabetical card file. (This last record may be done by the bride's mother after the wedding.)

These methods are perfect if a bride is moving to another city after the wedding, as she can take the card file index and the bridal gift book with her. Thank-yous are written in the order in which the gifts are received. By having the bridal gift book the bride has a record of that order and on the card file she has the donor's correct address and a second verification of the description of the gift.

The bride's mother keeps the enclosed gift cards for a third check.

ACKNOWLEDGMENT OF WEDDING GIFTS

THANK-YOU PAPER

The bride must use a fine quality plain or engraved note paper or informal for her thank-you notes.

If the thank-you paper is engraved or imprinted, it should carry the bride's name or initials only, never Mr. and Mrs.

If the bride is using engraved paper, it should be ordered at the same time as the wedding invitations or very shortly afterwards.

If some of the thank-you notes are to be written before the ceremony, and it is certainly wise to do this, some of the engraved or imprinted note paper should be ordered with the bride's unmarried name or initials, the remainder with her married name or initials.

[*] This third method should not be substituted for the wedding gift book record or for the record on the back of the enclosed gift cards. If only two records of the wedding gifts are required, it is better to use the bridal gift book and the record on the back of the gift cards.

WRITTEN BY HAND

All thank-you notes MUST be written by hand. No commercial thank-yous are acceptable.

WRITTEN BY THE BRIDE

All thank-yous are written by the bride herself, even if the wedding present is addressed to the groom and is from a relative or friend of the groom whom the bride has never met.

WHEN TO ACKNOWLEDGE

All wedding presents must be acknowledged as soon as possible after their arrival. A bride-to-be can usually keep up with her thank-yous until a few days before the ceremony, and it is important that she try to do this.

All wedding presents MUST be acknowledged, and no bride should wait longer than three months to do this, even though the wedding was very large and the gifts numerous.

If it is going to be impossible for a bride to acknowledge her wedding gifts within a reasonable time, a gift receipt card should be sent as soon as the gift is received. (Gift receipt cards will be explained later in this chapter.)

NOT WRITING THANK-YOUS

A bride-to-be should search her soul before deciding on the size of her wedding. Unless she is willing and capable of acknowledging personally the numerous gifts resulting from a large wedding, she should limit herself to the size she will or can handle graciously. Once she has decided to have a large wedding, she has simultaneously accepted the responsibility of personally writing many thank-you notes. It is inexcusable and rude not to write a thank-you note for every wedding gift received, no matter how small.

WEDDING TELEGRAMS

A verbal thank-you is all that is necessary for a wedding telegram.

HOW DOES THE BRIDE SIGN HER NAME?

Thank-yous for wedding gifts are signed Cordially, Affectionately, Sincerely, Love, etc.

The bride may sign only her first name if the sender of the gift is well known to her; if not she signs her first name, her maiden name, and her new surname, such as: Mary Jones Smith.

A THANK-YOU THAT WAS OVERLOOKED

The most careful person may overlook writing a thank-you, especially if the wedding was a large one and many gifts were received. If this happens and the bride hears about it, write or telephone the friend immediately explaining the oversight. Friends will understand and forgive.

ADDRESSING

When a gift has been sent by a married couple, the bride writes to the wife. Within the letter she thanks both the husband and the wife.

RETURN ADDRESS

A return address may be embossed or handwritten upon the back of the envelope.

GIFT RECEIPT CARD

If the bride and groom are going abroad or on a long trip where it will be impossible to write thank-yous for many months after the wedding, or if the wedding was so large that hundreds of gifts were received, necessitating a delay in completing the thank-yous, a gift receipt card is sent immediately after receiving the gift.

This card may be engraved or printed (engraved for the formal wedding), and it is mailed immediately upon receiving the gift.

This card is sent to inform the sender that her gift has been received and as soon as possible the bride will write a personal thank-you. A gift receipt card does not take the place of a personal thank-you note. Many times this card is used when a bride is absent from her home (at school, etc.) until a few days before the ceremony. In this case they are addressed and mailed by the bride's mother.

A gift receipt card reads:

> *Miss Doris Townes*   (before marriage)
> *or*
> *Mrs. Robert Arthur Bell*   (after marriage)
> *acknowledges with thanks*   (wishes to
> *the receipt of your wedding gift* acknowledge)
> *and will take pleasure in writing you*   (and will
> write a personal note
> of appreciation at an early date)
> *at an early date*

OPENING AND RECORDING GIFTS WHEN A BRIDE IS ABSENT

When a bride-to-be is away at school or for some other reason will not be at the place of the wedding until a few days before the ceremony, there must be some arrangement made for opening and recording the wedding gifts. Most brides have little time to do this if they arrive home only a few days before the ceremony.

Usually the bride's mother obtains permission from the bride and the groom to open all gift boxes upon arrival. After permission has been granted, the boxes are opened and each gift is recorded in the bride's gift book, a description of the gift is written upon the back of the enclosed gift card, and the card is fastened securely to the gift. The gift is then either replaced in the gift box or placed on a gift display table with the gift card.

In this case a "Gift receipt card" is sent by the bride's mother as soon as the gift is opened. See the section, "Gift Receipt Card," p. 134.

INFORMAL THANK-YOU LETTER

Dear Mrs. Davis:

John and I are delighted with the lovely lamp and know it will be simply perfect in our apartment. We both like brass, as you obviously must have known. The gifts will be shown the day before the wedding. I hope you will be able to come over then, if not before.

Please express our appreciation to Mr. Davis, too.

Affectionately,
Evelyn

FORMAL THANK-YOU LETTER

Dear Mrs. Armstrong:

The tablecloth, which we have just received, is lovely. The color is beautiful and matches our china perfectly. John and I appreciate your thoughtfulness. Please express our appreciation to Mr. Armstrong, too.

John has spoken of you and your husband frequently and I am looking forward to meeting you at the wedding reception.

Sincerely,
Evelyn Morris

FOR THE SENDER OF WEDDING GIFTS

WHEN IS A WEDDING GIFT NECESSARY?

When an invitation to a wedding reception is accepted a wedding gift is sent.

If an invitation to a wedding reception is declined no gift is necessary, although many times one is sent.

If an invitation is for a wedding ceremony only, there is no gift obligation.

A handwritten or verbal invitation is usually issued when the wedding is quite small and customarily includes a reception or breakfast afterwards. Since this type of invitation is usually issued to a few chosen friends and relatives, whether or not it includes a reception or breakfast afterwards, a gift is ordinarily sent.

An invitation to a home ceremony customarily includes a reception or breakfast afterwards so, unless the invitation is declined, a gift is ordinarily sent.

An announcement does not require a wedding gift.

GIFTS OF CHECKS, BONDS, STOCKS

If gifts of checks, bonds, or stocks are sent, they are made out in the bride's and groom's names.

TO WHOM ARE GIFTS ADDRESSED?

All wedding gifts sent before the ceremony are addressed to the bride; after the ceremony they are addressed to the bride and groom.

TO WHOM ARE GIFTS SENT?

All gifts are sent to the home of the bride, unless there is another address included in the invitation.

ENCLOSED GIFT CARD

A gift card with the donor's name, with or without a brief felicitation in ink, is included with the gift. The donor's address is included unless it is certain the bride already knows it.

WHEN MORE THAN ONE INVITATION IS RECEIVED WITHIN A FAMILY

If more than one reception invitation is received within a family, each invitation must be answered separately. If the invitations are accepted and a gift is to be sent, ordinarily only one gift is sent by the family as a whole. All names to whom the invitations were addressed are included in the enclosed gift card.

GIFTS SENT LATE

Gifts sent late in response to an invitation are sent to the bride and the groom and a brief note of explanation for the tardiness should accompany the gift.

Gifts sent after the wedding in response to an announcement of a marriage are sent to the bride and the groom.

MONOGRAMMED LINENS

See the discussion of this earlier in this chapter.

ENGRAVED SILVER

See the discussion earlier in this chapter.

GIFTS FOR ELOPERS, SECOND MARRIAGES, AND SECRET MARRIAGES

No gift is expected for any of these marriages but many close friends and relatives will send them.

HOSTESS GIFTS

Many times a hostess, who is entertaining for the bride-to-be, will wonder if she should present the bride with a small gift as a memento of the occasion. The giving of a gift at any time or for any occasion is a matter of personal choice, and certainly this is no exception. If a hostess wishes to present the bride with a small gift it is her privilege to do so, but none is expected of her. There is one exception: a hostess for the bridesmaids' party does often present the bride with a small personal gift if the hostess is someone other than the bride's mother.

SHOWER GIFTS

If an invitation to a shower is accepted a gift is expected. If an invitation to a shower is declined no gift is expected, although one may be sent.

GIFTS FOR ANNIVERSARIES

If an invitation to an anniversary party is accepted and unless the invitation states "no gifts please," a gift should be taken.

If an invitation to an anniversary party is declined no gift is necessary, but one may be sent.

WEDDING ANNIVERSARIES, FIRST THROUGH SEVENTY-FIFTH

1st ...... Paper, plastics
2nd ..... Cotton
3rd ...... Leather
4th ...... Linen, rayon, nylon, silk
5th ...... Wood
6th ...... Iron
7th ...... Copper, brass
8th ...... Electrical appliances or bronze
9th ...... Pottery or china
10th ...... Aluminum or tin
11th ...... Steel
12th ...... Linen, silk, nylon
13th ...... Lace
14th ...... Agate or ivory
15th ...... Crystal or glass
20th ...... China
25th ...... Silver
30th ...... Pearls
35th ...... Coral or jade

40th ...... Rubies or garnets
45th ...... Sapphires
50th ...... Gold
55th ...... Emeralds or turquoise
60th ...... Diamonds
75th ...... Diamonds

Chapter 15. Responsibilities and Expenses of the Bride, Groom, and Their Parents

All suggestions are general and may vary with location or local customs.

THE BRIDE'S RESPONSIBILITIES

Your parents are the first to be told of your engagement.

With your fiance select your wedding date, time, and particular type of wedding.

Consult your parents and together decide how much they are able to spend on your wedding.

Make an appointment for you and your fiance to visit your minister. Be there on time, dressed as you would if you were going to church.

Make out a list of your attendants; help the groom-to-be to select the ushers.

Decide upon the color scheme you want to use for your wedding.

Select your attendants' dresses and headdresses; it is a good plan to enlist the help of one or two of your attendants (not more, as too many ideas are confusing). Keep in mind the financial status of your attendants while making your selection and also the wearability of the dresses afterwards.

With your mother, order your invitations, announcements, and all enclosure cards. At the same time order thank-you note paper, plain if you like, or some with your unmarried monogram or name and some with your married name or monogram. Use only your engraved name (or initials) on thank-you note paper, never Mr. and Mrs., and DO NOT use commercial thank-yous under any circumstances.

Choose your china, crystal, and silver patterns at the store most likely to be patronized by most of your friends; the groom goes with you, if possible. If these patterns are selected at a bridal consultant store, you will find they will help with many of your wedding problems.

Choose your wedding veil and dress, usually with the help of your mother, and do enlist the services of a bridal consultant at your favorite store. Her services are free if you purchase your bridal finery at her shop and her assistance is invaluable.

Help with the wedding invitation list as much as possible. You and your fiance should make a list of all of your young friends to be invited to the wedding or to be sent announcements.

Address as many of the invitations as possible; you might recruit some of your friends or attendants to help.

Do get an engagement book and keep an accurate record of all party and other engagements and see that you arrive on time. For parties given in your honor, you arrive a little before the scheduled time. Write thank-you notes IMMEDIATELY to all hostesses entertaining in your honor. If you are sending flowers to your hostess, see that you have made arrangements for these to be delivered to her home.

See that all accounts of parties and wedding plans are sent or taken to your local paper, if these are being used by your newspaper.

Consult your florist, if possible with your mother. The questions you need to ask are listed in Chapter 19, "Your Florist."

Furnish each hostess who is entertaining for you a list of guests' names, being sure to ask how many names to include; DO NOT include more names on your guest list than the number your hostess specifies. Make out your guest list, complete with addresses and telephone numbers, as soon as she asks for it and either deliver it to her home or mail it IMMEDIATELY. Do not under any circumstances force a hostess to ask a second time for a party guest list. Write your hostess a thank-you immediately after the party. Send flowers either for or after the party, if you can afford it.

Select your attendants' gifts, and don't forget the flower girl, if there is to be one.

Select your gift to the groom.

Keep your wedding gift book up to the minute; record each gift as it is unwrapped; save all enclosed gift cards, writing on the back of each a description of the gift.

Keep up with your thank-you notes. THIS IS IMPORTANT. Write a few each day. You will find it pays later.

Shop for your bridal necessities.

With your groom-to-be shop for your house furnishings.

Select the music for your wedding and reception.

Make any hotel reservations for your out-of-town attendants. Their hotel bill is your (or your parents') responsibility.

Check with the groom to make certain his attire is all arranged; help him to select his attendants' gifts, and remind him to make any hotel reservations for his out-of-town attendants, family, or friends.

Plan your honeymoon with your groom-to-be.

Have your picture made in your wedding gown, and be sure to have a glossy print made for the newspaper.

Write a personal note to any out-of-town friends you especially want to attend your wedding.

If your future in-laws live in your city, call them occasionally, inviting them over to see the wedding presents and to discuss any new developments in the wedding plans. If they live in another city, drop them an occasional note telling of the wedding plans and any presents received from their friends. You can't imagine how much this little thoughtful gesture will mean to them.

Assist in arranging the gift display; checks are not displayed. See Chapter 14, "Wedding Gifts."

If your state requires a doctor's certificate, make an appointment with your doctor, and if your groom is from out-of-state, you may have to make one for him also.

Have a dental check.

If you wish to keep a scrapbook, keep all newspaper accounts of parties and prewedding festivities as they appear, putting the clippings into a box. They may be pasted in a book later.

If you are giving the bridesmaids' party, make arrangements for this.

Make a memo of much-used telephone numbers; keeping it handy will save many minutes.

Select, with the groom, two ushers to unroll the bridal carpet and two ushers to unroll and fasten the aisle ribbons. (The same two may be used for both duties, but if there are enough ushers it is thoughtful to use two different pairs.)

Select, with the groom's mother and your mother, an usher to escort each of them at the church.

Choose one or two of your close friends to keep the bridal book at the reception. Help your mother make out a list of friends who are assisting at the reception.

For receiving-line thank-yous memorize as many of the gifts and donors as possible.

Make an appointment at the beauty shop.

Go with your groom to get your marriage license.

Do your own packing for your wedding trip.

Take part in your wedding rehearsal.

Plan to wear something old, something new, something borrowed, and something blue.

Drive to the church with your father only or with your father and a chauffeur and do try not to sit on your wedding gown.

Take your father's right arm in the processional unless your minister specified otherwise.

If your groom is from out-of-town, see that he meets everyone as they come through the receiving line.

Toss your bridal bouquet with your eyes closed.

Don't forget to tell your parents and the groom's parents goodbye before leaving for your honeymoon.

Send a telegram of thanks to both parents after the wedding.

Have a WONDERFUL honeymoon.

THE GROOM'S RESPONSIBILITIES

All suggestions are general and may vary with location or local custom.

Tell your parents of your engagement and approaching marriage.

Call on the bride's father as soon as possible after the bride has told him of the engagement.

Choose the engagement and wedding rings. Your bride is usually consulted here.

With the bride select a tentative wedding date and time (this must be approved by the minister). Choose the type of wedding. The formality of the wedding depends upon the type of wedding dress the bride chooses.

Go with your bride for a visit to the minister.

Choose your best man and your ushers, the latter with your bride's assistance. Inform the men of attire to be worn.

Shop with your bride to select your silver, china, and crystal patterns, if you wish.

Select and purchase the proper clothes to be worn at the wedding. See Chapter 18, "Dress for Weddings."

Supply the bride's mother with a complete list of the names and addresses of your friends and relatives for the wedding invitations or announcements.

Offer as much help as possible to the bride's mother.

With the bride, consult the florist. Flowers for which you are responsible are listed in Chapter 19, "Your Florist." Don't forget your bride's going-away corsage.

Select with the bride two ushers to unroll the bridal carpet, and two to draw and fasten the aisle ribbons. (The same two may be used for both duties; but if there are enough ushers it is thoughtful to use two different pairs.)

Choose, with the bride and your mother's approval, an usher to escort your mother at the church.

Obtain health certificate. This must be done before you can secure your marriage license.

Allow plenty of time for the marriage license to be issued. In addition to medical certificates there may be other documents that must be submitted. It is best to call the registrar for specific information as to what is required. The marriage license must be issued in the same state and many times in the same county in which the ceremony is to be performed.

Shop with the bride for any furniture needed for your new home.

If your parents live in another city, keep them posted on all wedding plans.

Select gifts for the best man and ushers. If there is a ring bearer, he is given a small remembrance. Purchase your gift for the bride. Gifts are presented to the ushers and best man at the bachelor party if there is one. If there is no bachelor party, gifts are presented at the rehearsal party or a few days before the ceremony. See Chapter 14, "Wedding Gifts," for suggestions.

Be on time for all parties given in your honor; especially be on time for your rehearsal and ceremony.

Give the bride's mother a list of all your out-of-town friends and relatives who are planning to attend the wedding. She will need these names for party lists and for the seating arrangements at the church.

Make hotel reservations for any out-of-town attendants; their hotel bills are your responsibility.

Make hotel reservations for your parents or any other out-of-town relatives who are attending your wedding; their hotel bills are their responsibility.

Entertain your attendants and any other friends at a bachelor party if possible.

With the assistance of the best man, make all out-of-town reservations and transportation arrangements for the honeymoon.

If the wedding presents are to be shipped after the wedding, make these arrangements. The charges are your responsibility.

If you are moving into a new home after the honeymoon, notify the utility, electric, and telephone companies when to start service.

Change your life and accident insurance to your new beneficiary. Make certain to have hospitalization insurance for both of you.

Obtain travelers checks to cover all expenses of the wedding trip.

Give your best man the minister's fee and the wedding ring before the ceremony.

If you are wearing gloves at the ceremony, take them off and hand them to the best man as the bride starts down the aisle.

SMILE, SMILE, SMILE as your bride comes down the aisle.

After the ceremony, if toasts are being offered, follow the best man's first toast with a toast to your new bride.

Cut the first slice of wedding cake with your bride, your right hand over her right hand.

Don't forget to tell your parents and the bride's parents goodbye before leaving for the honeymoon.

Send a telegram or note of thanks to both sets of parents after the ceremony.

Any personal gifts to you are acknowledged by you.

Sign the hotel register Mr. and Mrs. Thomas Harris, not Mr. Harris and wife.

Have a WONDERFUL honeymoon.

THE BRIDE'S PARENTS' RESPONSIBILITIES

All suggestions are general and may vary with location or local custom.

Consult your minister, with the bride if possible. If the bride cannot make the call with you, you may go alone or with your husband. Questions to ask him are listed in Chapter 3, "Consulting Your Minister."

With the bride and groom decide when and where the wedding reception or breakfast is to be held. Contact said place before ordering the invitations to make certain that the date and time are available and the reception can be scheduled. If the reception or breakfast is to be held at home and a catering service is being used, it must be contacted and the date and time engaged before the invitations can be ordered.

Make all plans for the wedding (see Chapter 2, "Types of Weddings") and for the reception (see Chapter 22, "The Reception").

Order invitations, announcements, and enclosure cards with the bride's assistance.

Compile the invitation and announcement list. Address, stamp, and mail all invitations. The bride and other members of the family help. Announcements are mailed after the ceremony.

Help the bride choose her china, crystal, and silver patterns if she expresses a desire to have you do so.

Help the bride choose her wedding trousseau and attendants' dresses if she expresses a desire to have you do so.

Keep a calendar of events; keep it up to date.

Select your clothes and help your husband in his selection.

Consult your florist; questions to ask are listed in Chapter 19, "Your Florist."

Make arrangements for any pictures that are to be taken during and after the ceremony.

If you have engaged a caterer for your reception or breakfast, make an appointment with him to select your menu, etc. If you have engaged a club or hotel dining room or ballroom for your reception or breakfast, make an appointment with the dining room manager to select your menu, etc.

If you would like a recording of the ceremony and your church allows this, arrangements can be made for it. Private recording studios are listed in the yellow pages of your telephone directory.

Make reservations for out-of-town relatives and friends; they pay their own hotel bills.

Make arrangements for billeting any out-of-town attendants to the bride; their hotel bills are your responsibility.

If the groom and his family are from out-of-town, the bride's mother will make their hotel reservations. If the groom's family is from out-of-town and the groom is living in the same city as the bride, it is the groom's responsibility to make their hotel reservations; the bride's mother might remind him of this, however. The groom and his parents pay their own hotel bills.

If the groom and his attendants and his family are from out of town the bride's mother makes all their hotel reservations. The cost is the obligation of the groom's family.

If the wedding presents are many, engage a policeman or private detective to guard them while the family is at the ceremony.

Contact the insurance company and have them issue a floating poli, on the wedding presents while they are in your home.

Arrange for any extra household help you might need.

Make a list of friends you wish to assist at the reception. Write or telephone each. You might ask one special friend to help you make out your list of assistants. See Chapter 22 on "The Reception" for further suggestions.

If the groom's parents live in your city, call them occasionally and invite them over to see the wedding gifts. Their friends are sending wedding gifts also, and it is only fair that they know what their friends have sent as well as share in this happy part of the wedding. If the groom's parents live in another city, it is considerate to occasionally send them a list of the wedding gifts, especially those sent by their friends.

Arrange for transportation for the bridal party and out-of-town relatives and friends to the church and from the church to the place of the reception. Remember the bride's father rides with her to the church, so make certain there is room for him to ride with you to the place of the reception.

If the groom's parents are from out of town, write his mother a description of your dress and the type of attire your husband is wearing.

Contact the police department if your wedding is to be a large one and ask if they will reserve a parking section in front of the church for the wedding cars.

Make certain there are sufficient parking facilities at the church for guest cars.

Make arrangements for the displaying of the wedding gifts; ideas are given in Chapter 14, "Wedding Gifts."

Be sure the time and the date of the wedding rehearsal are clear to everyone concerned.

If you live out in the country, you might send a map of the route to all guests who are coming from out of town.

Consult with the bride and the groom as to whether there is to be a special usher to seat you and the groom's mother at the church. You might also make certain the bride and groom have asked ushers to unroll the bridal carpet and the aisle ribbons.

Order, at least four weeks before the ceremony, your bridal napkins, match folders, decorated candles, and any other bridal effects that are to be used. A complete list may be found in Chapter 22, "The Reception."

Two weeks before the ceremony order the wedding cake and the boxed groom's cake, if this is being used.

The bride's mother generally attends all parties given for the bride.

Assist the bride in opening and recording the wedding gifts. Recording is explained in Chapter 14, "Wedding Gifts."

Record all replies to reception invitations.

Send a few extra invitations to the groom's parents if they reside in another city. If they reside in your city, see that they are given a few extra invitations.

Send all newspaper accounts of the prenuptial parties and events to the groom's parents if they live in another city.

Keep a memo of all much-used telephone numbers such as the florist, bridal consultant, bridal gift consultant, all attendants, caterer, the minister, etc. This will save endless time.

If there is to be a special seating arrangement at the church, such as pew cards or within-the-ribbons section, give this list to the head usher.

Engage someone to park cars if your reception is a large

one and is being held at home. If the reception is being held at a club or hotel, they will handle the parking, but you might ask about it.

If your reception is to be large, it is well to have a doorman, especially in the rainy season.

If the reception is large, engage a maid to take care of guests' wraps.

See chart for positions in the receiving line, p. 237.

Don't keep your guests waiting too long (while pictures are being made) before you receive them. Suggestions on how to avoid this are on page 252.

The bride's father may stand in the receiving line, or he may prefer not to do so. Either is correct.

If the groom and/or his parents live in another city, either send a copy of the wedding information directly to his hometown newspaper or give the information to the groom's mother so that she can have it placed in their newspaper.

Write thank-you notes to everyone who assisted you at the reception and the wedding.

Write thank-you notes to everyone who sent flowers for your daughter's wedding or reception.

THE GROOM'S PARENTS' RESPONSIBILITIES

All suggestions are general and may vary with location or local custom.

If you live in the same city as the bride, call upon the bride and her parents before the engagement is officially announced, showing your approval of the happy event.

If you live in another city, write a letter to the bride and the bride's mother, expressing your approval and happiness over the coming event.

If you live in another city, ask the bride if you may register her gift preferences with your leading store.

You may want to send the bride an engagement gift. A piece of family jewelry is most appropriate.

Send your invitation and/or announcement list, complete with addresses, to the bride's mother as soon as possible.

Send the bride's mother a list of your out-of-town relatives and close friends who will attend the ceremony and reception, so that seating arrangements can be made for them at the church and they will be included in any party invitation lists.

If you live in the same city as the bride's parents, offer your assistance during the wedding and reception preparations. You might assist with the addressing of the invitations and with plans for the reception.

When you and your husband plan and buy your own wedding attire, be sure they harmonize with the bride's parents' costumes.

You and your husband usually entertain for your son and his bride-to-be (after the engagement has been announced), especially if you reside in the same city. Although it is not obligatory, it is a gracious gesture for you and your husband to give the rehearsal party. If you plan to give this party, inform the bride's mother of your intention immediately. Even if you live in another city, plans can be made to entertain for the bridal couple, with the assistance of the bride's mother or by contacting the manager of a suitable club or hotel.

If you live in another city, make your own hotel or motel reservations. The bride's mother will supply the name of a suitable and convenient hotel or motel.

It is best to consult the bride and the groom before buying a wedding gift. Buy, of course, the finest wedding gift you can afford, but it should be their preference.

Attend all wedding parties to which you are invited. Not attending parties gives the impression that you do not approve of the match.

Arrive at the church at least twenty minutes before the scheduled time of the ceremony.

Take the usher's RIGHT arm and he will seat you on the right side of the church. Your husband walks a few paces behind you.

You are always in the receiving line at the reception. Your husband has a choice of being in the line or not.

If there is dancing, your husband dances with the bride (following the bride's dance with her father).

After the wedding write a letter to the bride's mother, telling her what a lovely wedding it was.

EXPENSES OF THE BRIDE

A gift for the groom.
The groom's ring if it is to be a double-ring ceremony.
Gifts for the bridal attendants.

Your bridesmaids' party, unless a relative or friend is giving this.

Your medical and dental examination.

Stationery used for personal notes.

Your thank-you note paper.

Your wedding gift book.

Your wedding guest book.

EXPENSES OF THE GROOM

Flowers (listed under "Flowers for which the Groom Pays," p. 189).

The engagement ring.

The wedding ring.

The wedding trip.

The marriage license.

A gift for the bride.

Gifts for the best man and ushers, and the ring bearer if there is to be one.

Gloves and ties worn by the best man and ushers.

Hotel accommodations for any out-of-town male attendants.

The fee to the minister.

The bachelor party, unless the best man or friends are giving this.

Any medical tests or examination.

Your wedding attire.

Any expense involved in the shipping of the wedding presents.

Your future home and all major equipment.

EXPENSES OF THE BRIDE'S PARENTS

The announcement party if you give it.

All invitations, announcements, and enclosure cards.

Flowers listed in Chapter 19, "Your Florist."

Stamps for mailing invitations, announcements, and personal notes.

All expenses of the ceremony, except those listed otherwise.

All expenses of the reception or breakfast following the ceremony.

The rehearsal party if you give it.

Fee for the sexton, organist, soloist, choir, acolytes, candle lighters, crucifer, or for any other staff members who assist with the ceremony at the home, club, or hotel, other than the minister.

A wedding gift for the bride and groom.

The bride's wedding costume and trousseau.

Your own personal attire and the attire of any other members of your family living at home.

Any recordings made of the ceremony.

Any photographs, pictures, or movies made at the ceremony or reception.

The bride's photograph made before the ceremony.

The wedding cake or cakes.

Music for the ceremony and the reception.

All food and liquid refreshment served at the reception.

Any insurance taken on the wedding gifts while they are in your home.

A professional to guard the wedding presents while you and your family are at the ceremony and reception.

Any bridal consultant or bridal secretarial charges.

Any extra help employed to assist with the wedding or the reception.

All catering charges.

Hotel accommodations for any of the bride's attendants.

Any transportation charges for the bridal party to the church and from the church to the place of the reception.

Gratuity to the traffic policeman.

Any expense involved in parking cars at the reception.

Stationery used for personal notes to friends.

Flowers sent to a hostess entertaining for the bride.

Any expense involved in the arrangement of the gifts.

The file and card file for the guest list.

Candle holders, candles, canopy, ribbons, aisle carpet, or anything rented or bought for the ceremony or reception or for the display of the wedding gifts.

If money is no object, payment for the bride's attendants' dresses.

EXPENSES OF THE ATTENDANT

Your wedding costume.

A gift for the bride and groom.

Any traveling expense.

The expense of any entertaining you do for the bride and groom.

Hotel accommodations for the bride's attendants are paid by the bride's parents.

EXPENSES OF THE GROOM'S PARENTS

Your wedding costumes and any other clothes you might need for the wedding festivities.

Your own traveling expenses and hotel bills.

Hotel accommodations for the groom's out-of-town attendants, unless the groom pays for this.

Any entertaining you might do for the bride and groom.

The loveliest wedding present you can afford for the bride and groom.

NOTE: All expenses are general and may vary with location or local custom.

Chapter 16. The Wedding Attendants, Their Duties and Responsibilities

All bridal attendants buy their own dresses and accessories. If money is no object, sometimes the bride's family pays for the bridal attendants' costumes. This is not expected, however. The bride's family furnishes bridal attendants' headdresses if they are made of flowers. They also furnish the bridal bouquets.

The groom's attendants buy their own attire. The groom furnishes their gloves, ties, and boutonnieres.

All attendants must attend the wedding rehearsal, and they are expected to be on time.

All attendants are expected to keep their fitting and party appointments.

All attendants send a wedding gift to the bride and groom, either as individuals, as a group, or with their parents.

Although it is not absolutely necessary, if possible attendants should entertain for the bride or for the bride and the groom.

Bridal attendants are invited to all parties given for the bride. Groom's attendants and bridal attendants are invited to all parties given for the bride and the groom. Groom's attendants are invited to all stag parties. (The exception to any of the above would be office parties or special group parties.)

A bride may have both a maid and a matron of honor, but she must decide which one will attend her at the altar.

Bridal attendants stand in the receiving line; ushers do not. The best man does not stand in the receiving line unless he is also the father of the groom. Children attendants do not stand in the receiving line.

THE MAID OF HONOR

The maid of honor is the bride's dearest unmarried friend or relative. If the bride has an unmarried sister of suitable age (fourteen or over), this should be her honor assignment.

The maid of honor may help to compile the guest list and to address invitations, and she assists the bride and her mother with any last-minute errands.

A bride may have a maid and a matron of honor. If the maid of honor is the attending maid (or the one who attends the bride at the altar), she precedes the bride and her father in the processional, arranges the bride's train at the altar, holds the bridal bouquet during the ceremony, and again arranges the train as the bride leaves in the recessional. See page 156.

If a double-ring ceremony is being used, the maid of honor is in charge of the ring for the groom until a specified time in the ceremony.

In the recessional, if the attendants are walking in couples, the maid of honor walks with the best man.

She stands next to the groom in the receiving line at the reception.

If the reception after the ceremony is seated, she sits on the groom's left.

When the bride and groom are ready to leave the reception, she helps the bride dress in her going-away costume. See page 154.

MATRON OF HONOR

The matron of honor is the bride's dearest married friend or relative. If the bride has a married sister, this should be her honor assignment.

Duties of the matron of honor are the same as those of the maid of honor.

If both a maid and a matron of honor are being used, the bride must decide which one will attend her at the altar. The one attending will walk directly in front of the bride and her father in the processional (unless there is a flower girl and/or a ring bearer). If the bridesmaids are walking in pairs, the maid and the matron of honor may walk together and as they approach the altar the attending maid or matron will stand nearer the bride and hold the bridal bouquet, etc. See page 155.

BRIDESMAIDS

Bridesmaids are the bride's unmarried or married friends, sisters, or relatives of the bride or of the groom. If the groom has a sister of suitable age, although it is not necessary to invite her to be an honor attendant, it is customary to have her as a bridesmaid, especially if the wedding party is large.

The bride decides how many bridesmaids she desires at her wedding. Five or six seem to be the general rule; and if the wedding is more simple, there may be one honor attendant and one or two bridesmaids.

The bridesmaids either walk alone or in pairs in the processional, depending upon the wishes of the minister.

In the recessional the bridesmaids are usually escorted by the ushers; this again depends upon the wishes of the minister.

They stand in the receiving line at the reception, greeting the guests and giving their names to anyone who might not know them.

If the reception is seated, bridesmaids sit at the bride's table alternately with the ushers. See page 154.

JUNIOR BRIDESMAIDS

Junior bridesmaids are usually sisters or relatives of either the bride or the groom between the ages of twelve and fourteen.

Their duties and obligations are the same as those of the bridesmaids, except they do not entertain for the bridal pair.

FLOWER GIRL

The flower girl is a small child related to either the bride or the groom or the child of a best friend.

Sometimes she carries a tiny basket of flower petals which she strews in the aisle in front of the bride.

She walks directly in front of the bride in the processional.

If she is in the recessional, she walks directly behind the bride and the groom.

She wears a garland of flowers in her hair or some other kind of headdress.

She wears a party dress or a replica of the bridesmaids' dresses.

She must attend the rehearsal.

Her parents are responsible for her wedding attire.

She is not invited to bridal parties but her mother is, and her parents are invited to parties for the bridal couple.

Her flowers and flower headdress are furnished by the bride's parents.

She may or may not be a part of the recessional.

She does not stand in the receiving line at the reception.

THE BEST MAN

The best man may be either the groom's brother, father, uncle, cousin, or a friend.

He sends a wedding gift to the bridal couple.

He usually entertains for the bridal pair, or he may give the bachelor party if other arrangements have not been made.

He helps with any hotel reservations for the honeymoon and sometimes makes arrangements to have wine or flowers awaiting the bride and groom upon their arrival at their first-night hotel.

He sees that the bride's and groom's luggage is packed in the going-away car and helps with any last-minute packing.

He takes the groom's going-away clothes to the place of the reception.

He wears the same attire as the groom, but his boutonniere is different.

He helps the bride's mother with any last-minute chores of the wedding.

He helps the groom dress for the ceremony.

He sees that the groom has the marriage license safely in his pocket.

He is in charge of the minister's fee, which the groom has given to him before the ceremony, enclosed in a white envelope. The best man may give the fee to the minister before the ceremony if he is taking part in the recessional.

He drives the groom to the church.

He carries the wedding ring in his vest pocket and hands it to the groom at the appointed time. He reminds the groom to remove his gloves when the bride starts down the aisle.

He is not part of the processional but enters the church with the groom to await the bride.

He is one of the witnesses who sign the wedding certificate.

If he is in the recessional, he escorts the active maid or matron of honor.

He usually drives the maid of honor and some of the bridesmaids from the church to the place of the reception.

He does not stand in the receiving line at the reception unless he is also the father of the groom, in which case he has a choice.

He sits to the bride's right at a seated reception.

He proposes the first toast to the couple at the reception and reads any congratulatory telegrams.

If there is dancing at the reception, he dances with the bride, both mothers, and as many of the bridal attendants and guests as possible.

Many times he is responsible for seeing that the guest book is signed.

He makes all arrangements for the "getaway car" if one is being used. He assists the couple in getting away and sees them off if they leave by train, boat, or plane.

He sees that the bridegroom's wedding clothes are taken from the place of the reception.

The Ring Bearer

The ring bearer is a small boy, usually a relative of the bride or the groom or the child of a best friend.

He carries the wedding ring on a small, white, satin pillow. If the real ring is being used, it is secured to the pillow by light silken stitches. Very often the real ring is not used as the child's youth makes this impractical.

If the real ring is being used, the ring bearer must stay with the wedding party until the best man unfastens the ring from the pillow. If the real ring is not being used, the ring bearer may leave the wedding party when it reaches the altar and join his mother in her pew.

The ring bearer usually takes no part in the recessional.

In the processional he precedes the flower girl, if there is one; if not, he walks directly in front of the bride and her father.

If the real ring is not being used, the best man is in possession of it as usual.

THE HEAD USHER

The head usher is responsible for seeing that ushers arrive at the church on time for the rehearsal and the wedding.

He takes the groom's and best man's boutonnieres to the vestry.

He obtains from the bride's mother any special instructions for the seating of guests in the reserved section. He informs the ushers of this seating plan.

He watches the seating at the church to see that guests are seated uniformly on both sides.

If ushers have not been selected by the bride and groom to perform the following special duties, the head usher appoints them at the rehearsal:

1... Light the candles (if ushers are to perform this duty).
2... Inform the groom when the bride arrives at the church.
3... Seat the groom's mother.
4... Seat the bride's mother.
5... Draw the aisle ribbons.
6... Pull back the aisle carpet.
7... Return for the bride's mother.
8... Return for the groom's mother.
9... Return for honored guests.
10... Untie the aisle ribbons.

USHERS

Ushers pay for their own attire except that furnished by the groom, which usually consists of their gloves and ties.

Boutonnieres are furnished by the groom and will be given to the ushers when they arrive at the church.

The number of ushers needed will vary with the wedding. There should be one for every fifty guests invited to the church and there must be one for each bridal attendant. If more ushers than bridesmaids are necessary for the seating of guests, some of the ushers need not take part in the processional.

All ushers wear the same attire. See Chapter 18, "Dress for Weddings."

All ushers attend the wedding rehearsal, and they must be on time.

Ushers should arrive at the church about one hour before the ceremony starts.

Ushers line up at the left of the door in the vestibule of the church; this enables them to offer the *right* arm to each lady guest as she appears.

Ushers are sometimes called groomsmen in military weddings.

If "pew cards" are being used, each usher should be furnished a list of guests to be seated in the reserved pews, although it would be rare that a guest would forget that he had been assigned to this honor section; reference to these lists is seldom made. (See the section on "Pew Cards," p. 164, later in this chapter.)

If "within-the-ribbons" section is being used (this is explained later in this chapter), each guest as she enters the church informs the usher that she is to sit in this special section (on the left side if she is a friend of the bride and on the right side if she is a friend of the groom). Guests in this section are seated according to their arrival at the church as no special seat is reserved here (unlike "pew cards" where a special seat is reserved for each guest), except for the bride's and groom's parents and dearest friends and relatives.

If a guest is not sitting in a special section in the front of the church as she arrives she should say whether she is a friend of the bride or of the groom so that she may be seated on the correct side of the church (the left side for the bride's friends, the right side for the groom's friends). If a guest fails to inform the usher on which side she is to sit, the usher may ask, "Friend of the bride or the groom?"

If after many guests have been seated the church seems unbalanced, the later arriving guests should be seated so as to balance the seating arrangement, regardless of the guests' status.

If no pew cards or within-the-ribbons cards are being used, there are still some seats set aside for the families and honored guests. A list of these should be given to the head usher.

If the groom is from another city, he and his parents would

know few people in the bride's home town, so as a courtesy to him and his parents, wedding guests who are not sitting in a special section should be seated equally on both sides of the church. Imagine a church completely filled on one side of the church and practically empty on the other!

Ushers should talk to guests in a very low voice as they escort them to their seats.

Ushers send the bridal pair a wedding gift, either as a group or as individuals.

Ushers are invited to all parties given for the bridal couple unless it is a special group party or a family party.

Ushers walk in pairs in the processional and escort the bridal attendants or walk in pairs in the recessional. If an usher escorts a bridesmaid, he offers his right arm unless it's a military wedding, when the maids are on the left.

After the recessional is over, the ushers return and escort the mothers and honored guests out of the church. The bride's mother leaves first, the father following. The groom's mother then leaves, the father following.

If the reception is to be held somewhere other than the place of the ceremony, ushers go to that place immediately after the ceremony, as pictures are usually made of the complete bridal party.

Ushers mingle with the guests at the reception; and if there is dancing, they take part in it, dancing with the bride, both mothers, the bridal attendants, and guests.

HOW TO ESCORT GUESTS TO THEIR SEATS

Ladies arriving with male escort

An usher offers his right arm to the lady guest, seating her in a special section if she is an honored guest or relative, either on the bride's or the groom's side of the church. If she is not an honored guest or relative and she does not specify, the usher asks if she is "a friend of the bride or the groom" and seats her accordingly. Her male escort follows a few steps behind. If several couples arrive together and there is a shortage of ushers at the time, an usher offers his right arm to the eldest lady and the other couples follow, ladies walking first. He then seats the couples together.

Ladies arriving together without male escort

An usher escorts each lady to her seat unless at the time of their arrival there is a shortage of ushers, in which case he offers his arm to the eldest lady, the others in the party following singly a few steps behind. The usher then seats each lady in the party.

Small children

Small children are not escorted by an usher; the usher escorts the mother, the children following a few steps behind.

Young ladies (between twelve and fifteen)

Young ladies are very flattered to be escorted by an usher. If, however, there is a shortage of ushers at the time of their arrival, they may take their seats unescorted or follow their parents who are being ushered.

Men arriving alone

An usher does not offer his arm unless the man is very aged and feeble. He does walk beside the male guest showing him his seat.

PARENTS' SIDES IN THE CHURCH

Parents, relatives, and honored friends of the bride are seated on the LEFT side in the front of the church. The front row or pew is for the bride's mother only, until she is joined by her husband.

Parents, relatives, and honored friends of the groom are seated on the RIGHT side in the front of the church. The front row or pew is for the groom's parents only.

If the church has two main aisles, the parents are seated in the center pew section, the bride's parents on the left side, the groom's parents on the right.

WHEN THE MOTHERS ARE SEATED

After all the guests have been seated (except the very late arrivals) and the processional is about to begin, the groom's mother is escorted to her seat by an usher chosen for this honor, the father following a step or two behind.

The bride's mother is the last person to be seated before the aisle canvas is laid and the processional starts. She is escorted to her seat on the right arm of an usher chosen for this honor. No other person is escorted to a seat after the bride's mother is seated. Any late arrivals take their seats at the back of the church.

One usher may be chosen to escort both mothers, or one may be chosen to escort the bride's mother and a different one to escort the groom's mother.

Aisle Ribbons

After the bride's mother has been seated, two ushers walk together up the aisle to the last row of the bride-and-groom reserved section; here ribbon has been folded and laid alongside the aisle posts. Together the ushers pick up the bundle of ribbons and walk with them the entire length of the aisle pews, placing them securely over the end of each pew post until all pews are enclosed. They then fasten the end of the ribbon to the last pew aisle post.

These ribbons are used to enclose only the unreserved section of the church and are highly practical in preventing confusion after the ceremony is over, as they restrain the guests from leaving until after the parents and honored guests have been escorted out of the church. After the ceremony is over and the bride's and groom's mothers and other honored guests have been escorted out of the church, ushers remove these ribbons and the remainder of the guests may leave. Aisle ribbons are used on only the center aisles, not on the outside aisles; and although some few guests will leave by the outer aisles before they should, most of the guests will remain seated until after the honored guests have been escorted out and the aisle ribbons have been removed.

These ribbons do not enclose the bride's and groom's reserved section.

The Bridal Carpet or Aisle Canvas

After the aisle ribbons have been made secure, the aisle carpet is unrolled. It has been placed at the foot of the chancel steps and is unrolled by two ushers who have been selected by the bride and groom for this honor, either the same two ushers who placed the aisle ribbons or another pair.

The aisle canvas or carpet is often supplied by the church or the florist or it may be rented from a bridal supply firm. Whoever supplies it must make certain it is the correct length for the church aisle.

The aisle canvas or carpet is unrolled just before the processional starts.

"Within the Ribbons"

This is a reserved section in the front of the church using the left side for the parents, relatives, and honored guests of the bride and the right side for the groom's parents, relatives, and honored guests. A few rows on either side will suffice.

The aisle posts of this section are decorated with flowers and ribbons.

Guests sitting in this section are escorted out of the church after the ceremony is over, and no other guest should leave until after these guests have been escorted out. The bride's mother is escorted out first with the father following, then the groom's mother with his father following, relatives are next, then honored guests.

See Chapter 8 on "Enclosure Cards" for form.

Pew Cards

It is very rare that pew cards are used for the complete seating arrangement of a church. If they are, however, they are presented to an usher by each guest as she enters the church. Unless a wedding is extremely large and so important that many uninvited guests might appear at the church, pew cards for the entire seating arrangement of the church are impractical, confusing, very difficult to manage, and would require the services of professionals to handle.

Pew cards may be sent for the bride's and groom's reserved section of the church. They are sent to these guests after an acceptance has been received. A list of these guests should be given to each usher, although it would be unlikely a guest would forget she had been assigned to this honor section and reference is seldom made to these lists.

See Chapter 8 on "Enclosure Cards" for form.

Chapter 17. The Wedding Dress, Attendants' Dresses and Accessories

BRIDAL CONSULTANTS

Many large department stores and specialty shops have their own employees who assist with all the details of the dress for weddings, including the bride's wedding gown and accessories, the bridal attendants' dresses and accessories, and also those of the mothers and of any other female member of the wedding party.

These bridal consultants can also give information as to the correct attire for the groom, his attendants, and any male member of the wedding party.

Bridal consultants are employed by these stores, and this service is offered free to the bride who purchases her wedding gown and accessories at such a store. It is a wise bride who chooses her bridal trousseau at a store with this service, as many details are handled by the bridal consultant, eliminating many last-minute chores for the bride or her mother.

Some very large department stores combine their "bridal consultant" department and their "bridal gift consultant" department (this department is explained on page 123), thereby making it possible for the bride to make her selection of silver, crystal, and china patterns at the same store and at the same time, with little inconvenience on the bride's part. These departments keep a record of all pattern preferences and the number of items sold, so there is little fear of duplication.

SELECTION OF THE DRESSES

The bride or the bride and her mother select the wedding dress and accessories, although if the mother of the bride does help the final choice should be the bride's.

The bride, the bride and her mother, or the bride and one or two of the attendants select the bridal attendants' dresses and accessories. It is better not to ask too many people to help with the selection of the bridesmaids' gowns as there would be too many opinions, which often results in confusion.

Consideration should be given to the financial status of the bridesmaids when selecting their costumes and something should be chosen that will be useful afterwards. It is also well to take into consideration the weight of the bridesmaids before making a selection and to choose a style that will look well on all of them.

If the bridesmaids' dresses are to be ordered, they should be ordered at the same time so there will be no variation as to color and detail.

If the wedding gown and/or the bridesmaids' dresses or accessories are being ordered, they MUST be ordered well in advance of the date of the ceremony. THIS IS IMPORTANT.

If the bridesmaids' dresses are being made by a dressmaker, they should all be made by the same person or group of persons so that every detail will all be the same.

THE CORRECT DRESS

Consult Chapter 18, "Dress for Weddings," for the correct dress.

COLORS

White and creamy white are the traditional wedding dress colors, but in the past few years pastels have been used more and more and are now just as correct. Vivid colors are not used for the formal, traditional wedding gown. Black is never used for any wedding gown.

Bridesmaids' dresses may be any color (except black), including bright red, which is used frequently at Christmas time and proves very effective.

PAYING FOR WEDDING ATTIRE

The bride's wedding gown and accessories as well as the wedding trousseau are paid for by the bride's parents. If the bride's parents are deceased, she usually pays for her own trousseau, wedding dress, and accessories unless other arrangements have been made by a relative or guardian.

The bride's attendants pay for their own dresses and accessories. If their headdresses are made of flowers, the bride's family pays for these. Many times the bride will present the attendants with matching pearls and the gloves to be worn at the ceremony. In some communities the parents of the bride elect to pay for the attendants' dresses and accessories. This is most unusual, however, and is not expected.

WEDDING VEIL

A formal wedding veil may be worn by a bride at her first marriage only.

A face or blush veil is worn by a bride at her first marriage only; this type of veil is NEVER worn by a widow or a divorcee.

The correct length veil for a particular type wedding is given in Chapter 18, "Dress for Weddings."

THE WHITE WEDDING GOWN

A white formal wedding gown may be worn by a bride only if this is her first marriage.

HEADDRESS

The bride selects her headdress and veil at the same time she chooses her wedding dress, the length of the wedding veil depending upon the formality of the wedding. See Chapter 18, "Dress for Weddings."

The bridesmaids' headdresses are usually selected at the same time as their dresses. The bridal department will have many styles from which to choose or they may be designed and made in the hat department.

Large picture hats are more expensive than some other type headdress. Headdresses made or ready-made from the bridal department are the least expensive and are very effective.

GLOVES

If the wedding gown has short sleeves, long gloves are usually worn. If the wedding dress has long sleeves, the bride has a choice of no gloves or very short ones.

Bridesmaids usually wear gloves with short-sleeved dresses; they may or may not wear them with long-sleeved dresses.

All attendants' gloves should be the same length and, unless the bridesmaids are wearing harmonizing colors with matching gloves, the same color.

If the bride wears gloves, the under seam of the ring finger is ripped so that the ring may be placed upon her finger.

At very formal ceremonies, if gloves are worn by the bride, her attendants, and the mothers, they are usually left on while the receiving line is intact at the reception. At less formal receptions they may be left on or removed.

HEMS

Hems on the attendants' dresses should all be the same distance from the floor.

FITTINGS

The bride makes and keeps her own fitting appointments.

The bridesmaids make their own appointments for fittings, and it is their duty to keep such appointments. Never should a bride or her mother have to remind an attendant of a fitting appointment.

The bride should have a fitting a few days before the ceremony, as most brides will lose a few pounds with all the last-minute hustle and bustle.

JEWELRY

If the bride wears jewelry it should be very plain and beautiful—a simple pin or clip or a lovely strand of pearls. She should never wear flashy earrings or heavily studded bracelets. If the attendants wear jewelry, it should be something dainty and small, never large, dangling earrings or lots of bracelets. All bridal attendants wear the same, or similar, type of jewelry.

WEARING THE ENGAGEMENT RING DURING CEREMONY

If the bride wishes to wear her engagement ring during the ceremony, it is worn on the ring finger of the right hand.

WEARING GLASSES

If the bride wears glasses she may wear them with her wedding dress. If friends are accustomed to seeing a girl with glasses, she will look most unusual without them.

DELIVERY OF DRESSES

Most shops deliver the wedding dress, pressed and ready to don, to the bride's home the day before the ceremony. If the wedding dress is delivered in a packing box it should be removed immediately and hung up so that it will not become deeply creased and difficult to press.

Bridesmaids' dresses are delivered to their respective homes along with their headdresses, unless some other delivery place has been specified.

SHOES

Most brides wear white satin or lace slippers with their wedding gowns. There are many beautiful styles from which to choose, the height of the heel being a matter of choice. If the bride is wearing a pastel wedding gown, her slippers are usually dyed to match the gown.

Bridesmaids' slippers are usually dyed to match their dresses, and all bridal attendants should wear the same style and the same height heel.

HAIR

The bride and her attendants usually make hair appointments at the beauty shop for the day before the ceremony.

DRESSING

Allow plenty of time for dressing, especially if pictures are being made at home of the bride in her wedding dress. The maid of honor helps the bride dress. After the wedding dress is donned, avoid sitting down on it, if possible, until it is time to ride to the church; even then it is possible to sit upon the petticoat instead of the dress, thus avoiding a badly wrinkled wedding dress.

If the bride prefers to do so and there is a place provided, she and her attendants may dress at the church. In this case all bridal bouquets, dresses, and accessories are delivered to the church.

WEARING BLACK

Black is not worn by a bride at any type wedding.

Chapter 18. Dress for Weddings

BRIDE

Dress	Full length with cathedral or shorter train. White, creamy white, or pale tint. Long or short sleeves.
Shoes	Satin or lace, white or dyed to match pale tinted dress.
Veil	Long or finger tip, blush veil if desired.
Gloves	Long or short with short-sleeved dress. Short or none with long sleeves.
Bouquet	The bride's choice, or adorned prayer book.
Hose	Pale tint.
Jewelry	Real, nothing too ornate.
Headdress	To match veil and gown.

BRIDAL ATTENDANTS

Dress	Long or ballerina length. All the same style but harmonizing colors may be used. Attendants may wear shorter length even if bride's gown is floor length. All attendants' dresses must be the same length.
Shoes	Dyed to match dress. All wear the same style.
Headdress	To match gowns; cap, hat, or floral.

170

Gloves	If dress has short sleeves, gloves or mitts are worn. Optional with long-sleeved dress.
Bouquet	The bride's choice.
Hose	Pale tint.
Jewelry	Conservative, all alike or similar.

FLOWER GIRL

Dress	Dressy party dress or one to match bridal attendants' dresses.
Shoes	Dressy party slippers, white kid or black patent.
Headdress	Flowers or cap to match dress.
Gloves	Usually none. Mitts may, however, be worn.
Bouquet	Basket of flower petals or nosegay.

MOTHERS

Floor or cocktail length dressy afternoon gowns. Long or short sleeves. Black is never worn. Gloves of proper length and material. Dressy slippers or dyed to match gown. Suitable headdress. Jewelry. Corsage.

WOMEN GUESTS

Relatives and honored guests wear the same length dress as the mothers. Other guests wear long or shorter length. Suitable headdress. Gloves.

GROOM AND BEST MAN

Jacket	Winter—cutaway of Oxford grey or black. Summer—cutaway or stroller coat.
Trousers	Winter—black or grey striped. Summer—grey striped.
Waistcoast	Winter—grey striped. Summer—white linen.
Shirt	White starched bosom. Wing or turndown collar.
Hose	Black.
Tie	Grey ascot or four-in-hand, small figures or stripes.
Shoes	Black calf Oxfords, plain toe.
Top Coat	Dark Chesterfield.

Hat	Silk.
Scarf	White or grey.
Gloves	Grey.
Spats	Optional, usually none.
Handkerchief	White linen.
Suspenders	Grey or black and white.
Boutonniere	Groom—lily of the valley. Best man—gardenia.

GROOM'S ATTENDANTS AND FATHERS

Ushers and fathers dress like the groom and best man; ties may vary in color or stripe and trousers may be lighter or darker tone. Fathers' boutonnieres—white gardenias. Ushers' boutonnieres—white carnations. Wing collar is usually worn by groom and best man.

MALE GUESTS

Follow the dress status of the groom and best man or grey stroller coats and striped trousers. In more casual communities dark business suits are worn.

MILITARY GROOM, BEST MAN, ATTENDANTS, AND FATHERS

Wear regulation summer or winter dress uniform, the type prescribed by their particular branch of service and governed by the selection of the groom. No boutonnieres.

MILITARY GUESTS

Military guests dress the same as other male guests if regulations permit; if not they wear regulation summer or winter dress uniform, the type prescribed by their particular branch of service.

RING BEARER

A dark suit for winter. A white suit for summer.

Ultra-Formal—Evening—Six or After

BRIDE

Dress	Full length; creamy white, white, or pale tint. Long or short sleeves. Cathedral or shorter train.
Shoes	White satin or lace or dyed to match pale tint dress.
Veil	Full length, blush veil if desired.
Gloves	Optional with long sleeves, long or short gloves may be worn with short sleeve dress. White kid or to match dress.
Bouquet	The bride's choice or adorned prayer book.
Hose	Pale tone.
Jewelry	Real, nothing too ornate.
Headdress	To match veil and gown.

BRIDAL ATTENDANTS

Dress	Floor or ballerina length. Attendants may wear harmonizing colors; but all attendants' dresses must be the same length, although attendants may wear shorter length even though the bride is wearing a long gown.
Shoes	Dyed to match gowns, all the same style.
Headdress	Cap or floral to match gowns.
Gloves	Gloves are worn usually if dress has short sleeves. All wear the same style. White kid or tinted to match gowns.
Jewelry	All the same or similar, nothing elaborate.
Bouquet	The bride's choice.

FLOWER GIRL

Dress	Party dress or one to match bridal attendants' dresses.
Shoes	Black patent, white kid, or party slippers.
Headdress	Flowers or tiny cap.
Gloves	Usually none, tiny mitts are sometimes worn.
Bouquet	Tiny nosegay or basket of flower petals.

MOTHERS

Floor-length conservative evening or dinner gowns. Long or short sleeves. Black is never worn. Gloves of proper length and material. Real jewelry. Headdress suitable for costume. Evening slippers. Corsage.

WOMEN GUESTS

Conservative evening or dinner gowns. Relatives' and honored guests' gowns should be the same length as those of the mothers'; other guests may wear shorter dresses if desired. Hats or suitable head covering. Gloves. Jewelry.

GROOM AND BEST MAN

Jacket	Tailcoat, black or midnight blue.
Trousers	To match jacket.
Waistcoast	Single or double breasted white pique.
Shirt	White, starched bosom with wing collar.
Hose	Black.
Tie	White.
Shoes	Black patent Oxfords or pumps.
Top Coat	Dark Chesterfield.
Hat	Silk opera.
Scarf	White silk.
Gloves	White.
Spats	Optional, usually none.
Handkerchief	White linen, monogram in white.
Suspenders	Grey or black and white.
Boutonniere	Groom—white lily of the valley. Best man—white gardenia.

GROOM'S ATTENDANTS

Ushers all dress alike, full evening attire the same as the groom and best man. Boutonnieres—white carnations.

FATHERS

Fathers follow the dress status of the groom and best man. Boutonnieres—white gardenias.

MALE GUESTS

In formal communities all male guests dress the same as the groom and the best man. In less formal communities dinner jackets are worn. In simpler communities dark conservative business suits are worn.

MILITARY GROOM, BEST MAN, ATTENDANTS, AND FATHERS

Wear regulation summer or winter dress uniform, the type prescribed by their particular branch of service and governed by the selection of the groom. No boutonnieres.

MILITARY GUESTS

Military guests dress the same as other male guests if regulations permit; if not they wear regulation summer or winter dress uniform, the type prescribed by their particular branch of service.

RING BEARER

A dark suit for winter. A white suit for summer.

FORMAL—DAYTIME—BEFORE SIX

BRIDE

Dress	Floor length. White, creamy white, or pale tint. Cathedral or sweep train. Long or short sleeves.
Shoes	Satin or lace. White or dyed to match pale tint dress.
Veil	Finger tip or longer if preferred; blush veil may be worn.
Gloves	Optional. Gloves are usually worn if dress has short sleeves. White kid or matching pale tint dress.
Bouquet	The bride's choice, or adorned prayer book.
Hose	Pale tone.
Jewelry	Conservative.
Headdress	To match veil and gown.

BRIDAL ATTENDANTS

Dress
: Floor or ballerina length. Dresses may be shorter than bride's but all attendants' dresses must be the same length. Harmonizing colors may be used.

Shoes
: Dyed to match the gowns, all the same style.

Headdress
: To match gowns; cap, floral, or hat.

Gloves
: If dress has short sleeves, gloves or mitts are worn. Optional with long sleeves.

Bouquet
: The bride's choice.

Hose
: Pale tone.

Jewelry
: Conservative, and all bridal attendants wear the same or similar.

FLOWER GIRL

Dress
: Dressy party dress or one to match bridal attendants' dresses.

Shoes
: White kid, black patent, or party slippers.

Bouquet
: Basket of flower petals or tiny nosegay.

MOTHERS

Dressy afternoon gown, long or shorter length. Long or short sleeves. Head covering suitable for costume. Dressy slippers. Gloves. Conservative jewelry. Corsage. Black is never worn.

WOMEN GUESTS

Relatives and honored guests wear dresses the same length as those of the mother; other women guests may wear long or shorter length. Accessories to match. Head covering in most churches.

GROOM AND BEST MAN

Jacket
: Winter—cutaway of Oxford grey or black. Summer—cutaway or stroller coat.

Trousers
: Winter—black or grey striped. Summer—grey striped.

Waistcoat
: Winter—grey flannel. Summer—white linen.

Shirt	White, pleated, or plain bosom. Wing or turndown collar.
Hose	Black.
Tie	Grey ascot or four-in-hand, small figures or stripes.
Shoes	Black calf Oxford, plain toe.
Top Coat	Dark Chesterfield.
Hat	Silk.
Scarf	White or grey.
Gloves	Grey.
Spats	Optional, usually none.
Handkerchief	White linen.
Suspenders	Grey or black and white.
Boutonniere	Groom—white lily of the valley. Best man—white gardenia.

GROOM'S ATTENDANTS AND FATHERS

Dress the same as the groom and best man. Ushers all dress alike but ties may vary in pattern and gray tone of trousers may vary. Wing collar is usually only worn by groom and best man. Ushers' boutonnieres—white carnations. Fathers' boutonnieres—white gardenias.

MALE GUESTS

Follow the dress status of the groom or wear dark conservative business suits.

MILITARY GROOM, BEST MAN, ATTENDANTS, AND FATHERS

Wear regulation summer or winter dress uniform, the type prescribed by their particular branch of service and governed by the selection of the groom. No boutonnieres.

MILITARY GUESTS

Military guests dress the same as the groom and best man if regulations permit; if not they wear regulation summer or winter dress uniform, the type prescribed by their particular branch of service.

RING BEARER

A dark suit for winter. A white suit for summer.

FORMAL—EVENING—SIX OR AFTER

BRIDE

Dress	White, creamy white, or pale tint. Floor length with short, sweep, or cathedral train.
Shoes	White satin or lace, or dyed to match pale tint dress.
Veil	Finger tip or longer. Blush veil may be worn.
Gloves	Optional with long sleeves; long or short gloves are worn with short sleeves. White kid or to match dress.
Bouquet	The bride's choice, or adorned prayer book.
Hose	Pale tone.
Jewelry	Real, nothing too ornate.
Headdress	To match veil and gown.

BRIDAL ATTENDANTS

Dress	Floor or ballerina length. Dresses may be shorter than bride's, but all attendants' dresses must be the same length. Harmonizing colors may be used.
Shoes	All wear the same style, usually dyed to match the gowns.
Headdress	To match gowns, floral or cap, all the same style.
Bouquet	The bride's choice.
Hose	Pale tone.
Jewelry	Conservative and all wear the same or similar.
Gloves	If dress has short sleeves, gloves are worn. Optional with long sleeves.

FLOWER GIRL

Dress	Party dress or replica of bridal attendants' dresses.
Shoes	White kid, black patent, or party slippers.

Headdress   A garland of flowers or headdress similar to those of the bridesmaids.

Bouquet   Tiny nosegay or a basket of flower petals.

MOTHERS

Floor length or shorter dinner or cocktail dresses. Long or short sleeves. Never black. Gloves. Suitable headdress. Jewelry. Evening slippers. Corsage.

WOMEN GUESTS

Conservative evening or dinner dresses. Relatives and honored guests should wear the same length gowns as those of the mothers; other guests may wear long or short length. Hats or suitable headdress. Gloves. Jewelry.

GROOM AND BEST MAN

Jacket	Tailcoat, black or midnight blue.
Trousers	To match jacket.
Waistcoat	Single- or double-breasted white pique.
Shirt	Starched bosom, wing collar.
Hose	Black.
Tie	White.
Shoes	Black patent Oxfords or pumps.
Top Coat	Dark Chesterfield.
Hat	Silk opera.
Scarf	White silk.
Gloves	White.
Spats	Optional, usually none.
Handkerchief	White linen, monogram in white.
Suspenders	Grey or black and white.
Boutonniere	Groom—white lily of the valley. Best man—white gardenia.

GROOM'S ATTENDANTS

Ushers all dress alike—full evening attire the same as the groom and best man. Boutonnieres—white carnations.

FATHERS

Fathers wear full evening attire, the same as the groom and best man. Boutonnieres—white gardenias.

MALE GUESTS

In formal communities all male guests dress the same as the groom and best man. In less formal communities dinner jackets are worn. In simpler communities dark conservative business suits are worn.

MILITARY GROOM, BEST MAN, ATTENDANTS, AND FATHERS

Wear regulation summer or winter dress uniform, the type prescribed by their particular branch of service and governed by the selection of the groom. No boutonnieres.

MILITARY GUESTS

Military guests dress the same as other male guests if regulations permit; if not they wear regulation summer or winter dress uniform, the type prescribed by their particular branch of service.

RING BEARER

A dark suit for winter. A white suit for summer.

SEMI-FORMAL—DAYTIME—BEFORE SIX

BRIDE

Dress	White, creamy white, or pale tint wedding gown; or white, creamy white, or pastel dressy afternoon frock resembling real wedding gown. Long or short sleeves. Ballerina or floor length. Short or no train.
Shoes	Dyed to match gown, or dressy slippers.
Veil	Elbow length or shorter.
Gloves	Optional, usually none.

Bouquet	The bride's choice or adorned prayer book.
Hose	Pale tone.
Jewelry	Conservative.
Headdress	To match veil or small bridal hat with short veil.

BRIDAL ATTENDANTS

Dress	Ballerina or street length. Long or short sleeves.
Shoes	Dressy slippers or dyed to match gown. All attendants wear the same style.
Headdress	Caps, circlets, or nose veils.
Gloves	Mitts to match gowns or short gloves.
Bouquet	The bride's choice, not too large.
Hose	Pale tone.
Jewelry	Conservative, and all attendants wear the same or similar.

FLOWER GIRL

Dress	Party dress.
Bouquet	Tiny nosegay or a basket of flower petals.
Headdress	Simple, either real or artificial flowers.
Shoes	Party slippers, white kid, or black patent.

MOTHERS

Dressy street-length gowns or suits. Hats if in church. Accessories to match gowns. Corsage. Jewelry. Gloves.

WOMEN GUESTS

Same as mothers. No corsage unless honored guest or relative.

GROOM, BEST MAN, ATTENDANTS, AND FATHERS

Jacket	Oxford grey or black stroller coat.
Trousers	Grey or black striped.
Waistcoat	Grey flannel.
Shirt	White starched or pleated bosom with turn-down collar.
Hose	Black.
Tie	Grey silk four-in-hand.

Shoes	Black calf.
Top Coat	Dark Chesterfield.
Hat	Black Homburg.
Gloves	Grey doeskin.
Boutonniere	Groom—white lily of the valley. Best man—white gardenia. Fathers—gardenias. Ushers—carnations.

MALE GUESTS

Same as the groom or dark conservative business suits.

RING BEARER

Dark suit for winter. White suit for summer.

SEMI-FORMAL—EVENING—SIX OR AFTER

BRIDE

Dress	Floor length or with sweep train. Long or short sleeves. White, creamy white, or pale tint.
Shoes	Satin or lace, white or dyed to match pale tint dress.
Veil	Elbow or finger tip length.
Gloves	Mitts or gloves matching dress, or white kid.
Bouquet	The bride's choice or adorned prayer book.
Hose	Pale tone.
Jewelry	Conservative.
Headdress	To match veil and gown.

BRIDAL ATTENDANTS

Dress	Floor or ballerina length, dresses may be shorter even though bride is wearing floor length. All attendants' dresses must be the same length. Harmonizing colors may be used.
Shoes	Dressy slippers or dyed to match gowns.
Headdress	Simple cap, circlets, or nose veils.
Gloves	Mitts or gloves matching dress, or white kid.
Bouquet	The bride's choice.

Hose	Pale tone.
Jewelry	Conservative, and all attendants wear the same or similar.

FLOWER GIRL

Dress	Party dress or replica of the bridesmaids' dresses.
Bouquet	Tiny nosegay or a basket of flower petals.
Headdress	Flowers or small net cap.
Shoes	White kid, black patent, or party slippers.

MOTHERS

Conservative dinner gowns or cocktail dresses. Long or short sleeves. Long gloves with short sleeves, short gloves with long sleeves. Suitable headdress. Jewelry. Evening slippers. Corsage.

WOMEN GUESTS

Same as mothers, no corsage unless honored guest or relative.

If the Dinner Jacket Is Being Worn When the Bride Wears a Formal Wedding Gown

As fashion changes for women, so it changes for men. Because of its coolness in the summer and since everyone seems to own one, the dinner jacket's popularity is growing by leaps and bounds.

The dinner jacket is SEMI-FORMAL attire and should never take the place of formal attire for an ultra-formal or formal evening wedding. In many localities we see them worn in great numbers, especially by the younger men, at the ultra-formal or formal evening wedding.

The dinner jacket is NEVER worn before six in the evening no matter where the location unless it is worn en route to a six o'clock wedding when the festivities will run later into the evening. If a wedding is before six, it is definitely not the garment to wear.

Local interpretation varies. In some communities the dinner jacket is considered more formal than in others. This would have to be taken into consideration before making any plans to wear the dinner jacket. If there is any doubt as to its correctness, a leading haberdashery shop should be consulted.

GROOM, BEST MAN, ATTENDANTS, AND FATHERS

Winter—Evening Only

Jacket	Midnight blue or black, single or double breasted.
Trousers	To match jacket.
Tie	Black or midnight blue bow tie.
Cummerbund	Black.
Shirt	Plain white or pleated front, two or three studs, wing or turndown collar.
Shoes	Black patent Oxfords or pumps.
Gloves	Grey.
Scarf	White.
Hose	Black.
Hat	Black Homburg or snap-brim felt.
Handkerchief	White.
Top Coat	Dark Chesterfield.
Boutonniere	Groom—white lily of the valley. Best man—white gardenia. Fathers—gardenias. Ushers—carnations.

Summer—Evening Only—After Six

Jacket	White shawl-collared. Midnight blue or black tropical worsted.
Trousers	Black or midnight blue evening trousers with the white shawl-collared jacket. Trousers matching jacket if dark jacket is worn.
Tie	Black or midnight blue bow tie.
Cummerbund	Black or midnight blue.
Shirt	Pleated bosom or plain white shirt.
Shoes	Black patent Oxfords or pumps.
Hose	Black.
Handkerchief	White.
Boutonniere	Groom—white lily of the valley. Best man—white gardenia. Fathers—gardenias. Ushers—carnations.

MALE GUESTS

Same as groom, or dark business suits. No boutonnieres.

INFORMAL—DAYTIME OR EVENING

BRIDE

Dress	White, creamy white, or pale tint wedding dress, ballerina length. White, creamy white, or pastel frock resembling real wedding gown, ballerina length. Street-length dress or dressy suit.
Headdress	Short veil, bridal hat, or small headdress.
Accessories	Small bouquet or prayer book. Dressy shoes. Gloves optional. Conservative jewelry. Pale tone hose.

BRIDAL ATTENDANTS AND MOTHERS

Dressy afternoon frock, same length as the bride wears. Street-length dress or dressy suit. Black is not worn. Hat or small headdress. Gloves optional. Conservative jewelry. Dressy slippers. Small bouquet or corsage.

GROOM, BEST MAN, ATTENDANTS, AND FATHERS

Winter

Dark blue suit. White shirt with turndown collar. Conservative four-in-hand tie. Black shoes. White handkerchief. White boutonniere.

Summer

White suit, or dark blue coat with white or grey trousers. White coat with blue or grey trousers. White shirt. Conservative four-in-hand tie. Navy socks. White shoes with white trousers, black shoes with dark trousers. White boutonniere.

Chapter 19. Your Florist

CHOOSING THE FLORIST

The florist should be chosen very carefully. A skillful florist will assist with every detail of the bridal flowers and the decorations at both the church and the place of the reception.

FLOWERS IN SEASON

Using flowers that are in season is far more economical than using rare and hard-to-obtain flowers that must be shipped a long distance. Flowers do not have to be the most expensive to be effective and beautiful. A good florist can make lovely arrangements no matter what flowers are chosen.

FLOWERS ON A BUDGET

If a budget is being followed and the florist is told approximately the amount that can be spent upon the flowers and decorations, he will come very close to keeping within this amount.

WHAT THE FLORIST MUST KNOW

The bride's name, address, and telephone number.
The date, time, and place of the ceremony.
The type of wedding.
The type and color of the wedding dress.
The color, size, and type bridal bouquet.

The color and type corsage for the bride's going-away costume.

The colors of the mothers' dresses and the kind of corsage to be sent to each.

The names, addresses, and telephone numbers of each attendant.

A material sample of the bridal attendants' dresses.

The type, color, and size of the bridal bouquets for attendants.

The style and type flowers for floral headdresses, if these are being used.

The petals or flowers for the flower girl.

The names and addresses of any female relatives or friends who are to be sent corsages; the color and type corsages to be sent.

The type boutonnieres desired for the groom, the best man, and the fathers.

The number of ushers and the type boutonnieres preferred.

Cushion for the ring bearer.

The kind of flowers to be used in the church decorations.

The aisle decorations at the church, including the number of aisles to decorate and the kind of flowers to use.

Whether or not aisle ribbons are being used.

Whom he can contact at the church for any additional information he might need about the church decorations.

The date, time, and place of the reception.

The kind of flowers to be used for the reception decorations.

The name and address of any hostess who is to be sent flowers for her party, the kind of flowers, the date and time to send them (sometimes flowers are sent as a courtesy to a hostess who entertains for the bride or for the bride and the groom).

The delivery time and place for all flowers for all attendants, family, and guests, and for the bride and the groom.

THE KNEELING CUSHION

The florist can supply the kneeling cushion for the church if the church does not have one.

THE AISLE CANVAS OR CARPET

The florist will supply the canvas runner for the aisle. The florist should measure the church aisle so as to make certain the aisle canvas is the correct length.

THE CANDLE HOLDERS

Extra candle holders are supplied by the florist if the church supply is limited.

AISLE DECORATIONS AND RIBBONS

The florist will make suggestions as to appropriate aisle decorations. If aisle ribbons are being used, he will supply these.

The florist will need to know the number of rows or pews that are to be included in the bride's and groom's reserved section of the church, so he can make the necessary decorations.

CANOPY

If a canopy is to be used and the church does not supply one, the florist will assist here.

DELIVERY OF FLOWERS FOR ATTENDANTS AND RELATIVES

Most florists deliver boutonnieres for the groom and male attendants and flowers for the flower girl to the church, and unless otherwise specified all other flowers are delivered to the respective homes of participants and guests. (Flowers for the bridesmaids are often delivered to the church.)

COLOR OF THE BRIDE'S BOUQUET

The bridal bouquet may be any color the bride prefers. The traditional bridal bouquet was formerly white with a touch of green, but many other colors are now used and are just as appropriate.

COLOR OF MOTHERS' AND HONORED GUESTS' CORSAGES

Colors of the corsages of the mothers, honored guests, and relatives should harmonize with their costumes. White, although permissible, is seldom used, especially if the bride is wearing all white.

COLOR OF THE BRIDAL ATTENDANTS' BOUQUETS

Attendants' bouquets should harmonize with their costumes, and they may all be the same or contrasting colors. Usually honor attendants' bouquets are a different color or larger than those of the other attendants.

FLOWERS FOR WHICH THE BRIDE'S FAMILY PAYS*

All flowers used in the decoration of the place of the ceremony and the reception.

Bouquets or corsages for the bridesmaids, honor attendants, and the flower girl. Their headdresses if they are made of flowers.

Corsages given to any friends who are assisting at the reception.

Flowers sent to any hostess entertaining for the bride or for the bride and the groom.

FLOWERS FOR WHICH THE GROOM PAYS*

The bridal bouquet for the bride.

A corsage for the bride's going-away dress or suit.

Corsages for the bride's mother and his mother and any other female relative or honored guest, such as grandmothers, aunts, cousins, sisters, etc.

Boutonnieres for himself, the best man, ushers, and fathers.

---

* In some communities the bride's parents pay for the bride's bouquet and going-away corsage, as well as the bridesmaids' flowers. This is most unusual, however. The above is the most usual procedure.

Chapter 20. The Rehearsal

THOSE WHO ATTEND

The presence of every member of the actual wedding party is of the utmost importance at the rehearsal. It should be made certain that each understands the date and the time clearly.

The organist and all members of the church staff who are assisting with the ceremony must also be present at the rehearsal. A call should be made to the church secretary to be certain they have been notified.

The bridal consultant should be notified of the time and date of the rehearsal, and she will be present to offer her services. Bridal consultants cooperate with the minister at the rehearsal and the ceremony but in no way interfere with the conduct of the service.

STAND-IN FOR THE BRIDE

Sometimes the bride prefers to use a stand-in at the rehearsal (called a mock bride). Although it used to be considered bad luck for the bride to take an active part in her wedding rehearsal, this old superstition has gone by the wayside, so that it is a matter of choice whether a stand-in is used or not.

IN THE EVENT AN ATTENDANT IS UNABLE TO SERVE

If a bridal attendant is unable to serve at the last minute, the grouping at the altar will have to be quickly rearranged.

DIFFERENT DENOMINATIONS

As there is such a wide difference among religious cere-monies of denominations and even among ministers of the same denomination, the minister will have to be the deter-mining factor in certain aspects of the ceremony. The minis-ter is the only one who can give instructions as to how the ceremony must be conducted, as he is the only one who knows and understands the many church rules by which he is governed. It would be impossible to give the exact pro-cedure for each denomination, as there would still be changes to be made. The following is the usual sequence, but there may be many changes a minister will want to make, as he may have an entirely different order to follow. Positions of the bridal party must be worked out with the minister.

The wedding rehearsal plays such an important part that it is very necessary for each member of the wedding party to be present at the rehearsal and to pay strict attention to every detail of the instruction from the minister. His wishes must be followed in every respect.

Chapter 21. The Church Ceremony

THE BRIDE

The bride and her father are usually driven to the church in a chauffeur-driven car. Sometimes their own car is used or a limousine is rented. (In large cities cars may be rented from a limousine service.) The bride's father does not usually drive, but sometimes this is his preference. The bride's car is parked in a reserved space in front of the church until she and her groom leave in it for the place of the reception.

The bride rides to the place of the reception with the groom, driven by the driver or chauffeur who drove her to the church. (If the father drove the car to the church, the groom drives to the place of the reception.)

THE MOTHER OF THE BRIDE

The mother of the bride leaves the house ten or fifteen minutes before the bride and may drive alone to the church or with any of the bridesmaids or relatives riding with her. More often, however, relatives drive her. Her car is parked in front of the church in a reserved space.

The father of the bride rides with the mother from the church to the place of the reception.

THE ATTENDANTS

If the bride's attendants dress or meet at the bride's home before the ceremony, some of them often ride to the church

with the bride's mother; others ride with relatives or friends.
If more cars are needed for the bridesmaids' transportation,
the bride's mother makes arrangements for extra cars. Spaces
are reserved in front of the church for the wedding cars.

The ushers usually take the bridesmaids from the church
to the place of the reception, the maid of honor riding with
the best man.

THE GROOM

The groom and the best man ride to the church together.
The groom and the bride ride to the place of the reception
together.

OUT-OF-TOWN GUESTS

Out-of-town guests either drive their own cars or the
bride's mother makes arrangements for their transportation.

PARKING AT THE CHURCH

If several spaces for the wedding cars are desired, the
police department should be contacted to make these arrangements. They are usually very happy to assist.

Nearly all churches have their own parking lots adjacent
to the church; if such space is not provided, arrangements
must be made in advance for the parking of guests' cars.

THE CHURCH CEREMONY PROCEDURE

THE USHERS

Ushers arrive at the church one hour before the scheduled
ceremony time. Their boutonnieres are at the church.

They are given last minute instructions by the head usher
on all final seating arrangements.

An usher offers his *right* arm to a lady guest.

See Chapter 16 for detailed instructions.

THE MUSIC

The music begins about thirty minutes before the ceremony.

THE CANDLES

The candles, if any, are lighted thirty to forty-five minutes
before the ceremony starts. (The minister is the guide here.)

THE BRIDESMAIDS AND HONOR ATTENDANTS

The bridesmaids and honor attendants, who either dress at home or at the home of the bride, arrive at the church and go to the room reserved for them. Frequently the attendants dress at the church. They are given their bouquets if the bouquets have been delivered to the church. See Chapter 16 for detailed instructions.

THE GROOM AND BEST MAN

The groom and the best man arrive at the church and go to the vestry where they are given their boutonnieres. See Chapter 16 for detailed instructions.

THE GROOM'S PARENTS

The groom's parents arrive at the church about twenty minutes before the ceremony is ready to start.

THE BRIDE'S MOTHER

The bride's mother arrives at the church about ten minutes before the bride.

THE BRIDE AND HER FATHER

The bride and her father arrive and join the bridesmaids.

SEATING OF RELATIVES

Relatives and honored guests are seated in the bride's section (on the left side) or the groom's section (on the right side).

SEATING OF THE GROOM'S PARENTS

The groom's mother, followed by the father, is escorted to her seat either by a special usher chosen for this honor or by the head usher. She takes the usher's right arm. The front row or pew on the right side is for the groom's parents only.

SEATING OF THE BRIDE'S MOTHER

Just before the processional starts, the bride's mother is escorted to her seat on the left side, by either an usher chosen for this honor or the head usher. She takes the usher's right arm. No one is escorted to a seat after the bride's mother is seated. Late comers must stand or take a seat in the rear. The front row or pew on the left side is for the bride's mother, where she is joined later by her husband.

THE AISLE RIBBONS

After the bride's mother is seated, two ushers (four if there are two aisles) stretch the pew ribbons.

UNROLLING THE AISLE CARPET OR CANVAS

After the pew ribbons have been made secure, two ushers unroll the aisle canvas (or carpet) which has been made ready and placed at the foot of the chancel steps. The processional is now ready to start.

THE SOLOIST

If wedding songs are desired, the soloist should sing just before the processional. Selections and timing are subject to the approval of the minister.

The Processional

THE ORGANIST

The organist starts playing the wedding march softly until the bride enters.

THE MINISTER ENTERS

The minister leaves the vestry and takes his place.

THE GROOM AND BEST MAN

The groom and best man follow the minister and take their places facing the center aisle.

THE BRIDE'S MOTHER RISES

In some churches, when the organist starts to play the wedding march, the bride's mother rises, which is a signal for all guests to rise. In some churches everyone remains seated. The minister is the guide for this.

THE USHERS ARE FIRST

The ushers are first, in pairs, the shorter ones followed by the taller. They divide at the chancel steps and arrange themselves on either side, an usher behind each bridal attendant.

THE BRIDESMAIDS FOLLOW

The bridesmaids follow, singly or in pairs, at not too rapid a pace. They divide at the chancel steps and arrange themselves on either side, a maid in front of each usher.

THE MAID OR MATRON OF HONOR

The maid and/or the matron of honor follow, singly or together. If there are two honor attendants and they walk singly, the active honor attendant is nearer the bride.

THE RING BEARER

The ring bearer comes next, walking behind the honor attendant.

THE FLOWER GIRL

The flower girl walks directly in front of the bride and her father.

THE ORGANIST

The organist increases the volume.

THE BRIDE AND HER FATHER

The bride enters on her father's right arm (unless there is some reason or the minister prefers the left arm).

THE GROOM'S GLOVES

The groom removes his gloves when the bride starts down the aisle. The best man reminds him.

THE GROOM SMILES

Since this is their happiest day, the groom should certainly smile as he sees his bride approaching the altar. The bride will treasure his smile always.

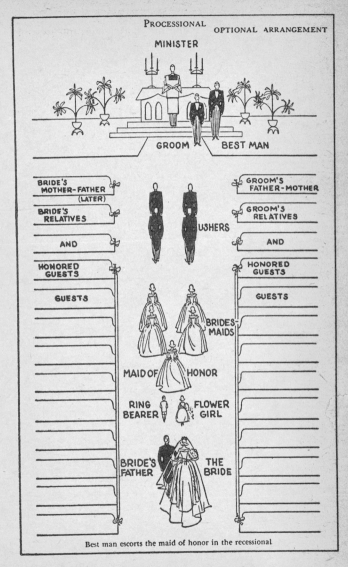

PROCESSIONAL

OPTIONAL ARRANGEMENT

MINISTER

GROOM — BEST MAN

BRIDE'S MOTHER–FATHER (LATER)

BRIDE'S RELATIVES

AND

HONORED GUESTS

GUESTS

GROOM'S FATHER–MOTHER

GROOM'S RELATIVES

AND

HONORED GUESTS

GUESTS

USHERS

BRIDES-MAIDS

MAID OF HONOR

RING BEARER — FLOWER GIRL

BRIDE'S FATHER — THE BRIDE

Best man escorts the maid of honor in the recessional

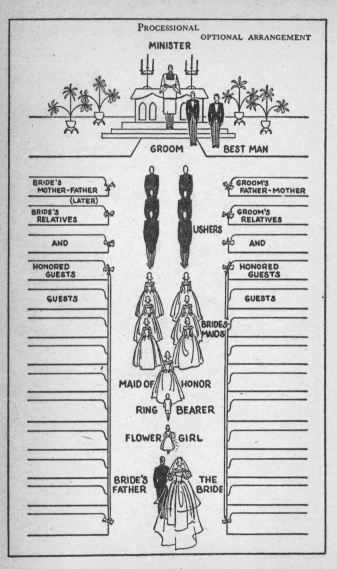

Processional

OPTIONAL ARRANGEMENT

MINISTER

GROOM   BEST MAN

BRIDE'S
MOTHER-FATHER
(LATER)

BRIDE'S
RELATIVES

AND

HONORED
GUESTS

GUESTS

USHERS

GROOM'S
FATHER-MOTHER

GROOM'S
RELATIVES

AND

HONORED
GUESTS

GUESTS

BRIDES-
MAIDS

MAID OF   HONOR

RING   BEARER

FLOWER   GIRL

BRIDE'S
FATHER

THE
BRIDE

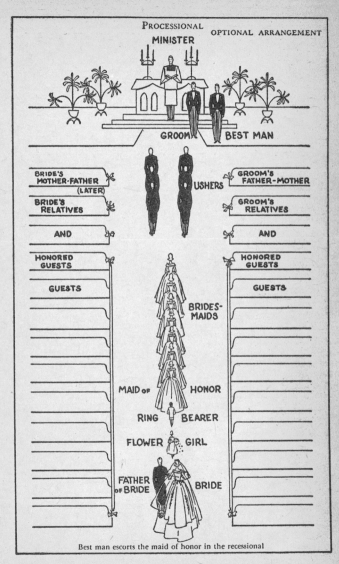

PROCESSIONAL — OPTIONAL ARRANGEMENT

MINISTER

GROOM — BEST MAN

BRIDE'S MOTHER-FATHER (LATER) — USHERS — GROOM'S FATHER-MOTHER

BRIDE'S RELATIVES — GROOM'S RELATIVES

AND — AND

HONORED GUESTS — HONORED GUESTS

GUESTS — GUESTS

BRIDES-MAIDS

MAID OF HONOR

RING BEARER

FLOWER GIRL

FATHER OF BRIDE — BRIDE

Best man escorts the maid of honor in the recessional

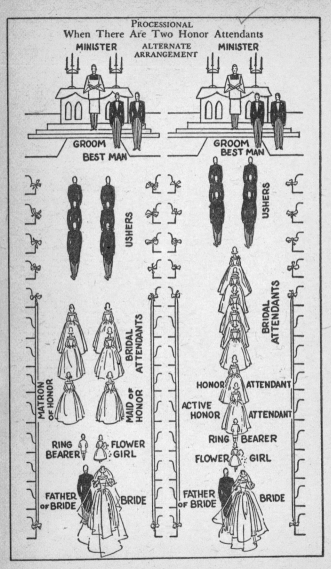

PROCESSIONAL
When There Are Two Honor Attendants

MINISTER · ALTERNATE ARRANGEMENT · MINISTER

GROOM · BEST MAN

USHERS

BRIDAL ATTENDANTS

MATRON OF HONOR · MAID OF HONOR

RING BEARER · FLOWER GIRL

FATHER OF BRIDE · BRIDE

BRIDAL ATTENDANTS

HONOR ATTENDANT · ACTIVE HONOR ATTENDANT

RING BEARER · FLOWER GIRL

FATHER OF BRIDE · BRIDE

ALTERNATE POSITIONS AT THE ALTAR

THE MARRIAGE CEREMONY

Many Protestant churches other than the Episcopal Church use the Episcopal Wedding Ceremony, which follows:

The Form of
Solemnization of Matrimony

At the day and time appointed for Solemnization of Matrimony, the Persons to be married shall come into the body of the Church, or shall be ready in some proper house, with their friends and neighbours; and there standing together, the Man on the right hand, and the Woman on the left, the Minister shall say,

DEARLY beloved, we are gathered together here in the sight of God, and in the face of this company, to join together this Man and this Woman in holy Matrimony; which is an honourable estate, instituted of God, signifying unto us the mystical union that is betwixt Christ and his Church: which holy estate Christ adorned and beautified with his presence and first miracle that he wrought in Cana of Galilee, and is commended of Saint Paul to be honourable among all men: and therefore is not by any to be entered into unadvisedly or lightly; but reverently, discreetly, advisedly, soberly, and in the fear of God. Into this holy estate these two persons present come now to be joined. If any man can show just cause, why they may not lawfully be joined together, let him now speak, or else hereafter for ever hold his peace.

And also speaking unto the Persons who are to be married, he shall say,

I REQUIRE and charge you both, as ye will answer at the dreadful day of judgment when the secrets of all hearts shall be disclosed, that if either of you know any impediment, why ye may not be lawfully joined together in Matrimony, ye do now confess it. For be ye well assured, that if any persons are joined together otherwise than as God's Word doth allow, their marriage is not lawful.

The Minister, if he shall have reason to doubt of the lawfulness of the proposed Marriage, may demand sufficient surety for his indemnification: but if no impedi-

*ment shall be alleged, or suspected, the Minister shall
say to the Man,*

.....Rudolph....Earl..... wilt thou have this
Woman to thy wedded wife, to live together after God's
ordinance in the holy estate of Matrimony? Wilt thou love
her, comfort her, honour, and keep her in sickness and in
health; and, forsaking all others, keep thee only unto her,
so long as ye both shall live?

The Man shall answer,

I will.

Then shall the Minister say unto the Woman,

.....Judith--Ann....Rose wilt thou have this
Man to thy wedded husband, to live together after God's
ordinance in the holy estate of Matrimony? Wilt thou love
him, comfort him, honour, and keep him in sickness and in
health; and, forsaking all others, keep thee only unto him,
so long as ye both shall live?

The Woman shall answer

I will.

Then shall the Minister say,

WHO giveth this Woman to be married to this Man?

*Then shall they give their troth to each other in this
manner. The Minister, receiving the Woman at her
father's or friend's hands, shall cause the Man with his
right hand to take the Woman by her right hand, and so
say after him as followeth*

I .... take
thee .... to my wedded
Wife, to have and to hold from this day forward, for better
for worse, for richer for poorer, in sickness and in health,
to love and to cherish, till death us do part, according to
God's holy ordinance; and thereto I plight thee my troth.

*Then shall they loose their hands; and the Woman
with her right hand taking the Man by his right hand,
shall likewise say after the Minister,*

I .... take
.... to my wedded

Husband, to have and to hold from this day forward, for better for worse, for richer for poorer, in sickness and in health, to love and to cherish, till death us do part, according to God's holy ordinance; and thereto I give thee my troth.

Then shall they again loose their hands; and the Man shall give unto the Woman a Ring on this wise: the Minister taking the Ring shall deliver it unto the Man, to put it upon the fourth finger of the Woman's left hand. And the Man holding the Ring there, and taught by the Minister, shall say,

WITH this Ring I thee wed: In the Name of the Father, and of the Son, and of the Holy Ghost. Amen.

And, before delivering the Ring to the Man, the Minister may say as followeth.

BLESS, O Lord, this Ring, that he who gives it and she who wears it may abide in thy peace, and continue in thy favour, unto their life's end; through Jesus Christ our lord. Amen.

Then, the Man leaving the Ring upon the fourth finger of the Woman's left hand, the Minister shall say,

Let us pray.

Then shall the Minister and the People, still standing, say the Lord's Prayer.

OUR Father, who art in heaven, Hallowed be thy Name. Thy kingdom come. Thy will be done, On earth as it is in heaven. Give us this day our daily bread. And forgive us our trespasses, As we forgive those who trespass against us. And lead us not into temptation, But deliver us from evil. For thine is the kingdom, and the power, and the glory, for ever and ever. Amen.

Then shall the Minister add,

O ETERNAL God, Creator and Preserver of all mankind, Giver of all spiritual grace, the Author of everlasting life; Send thy blessing upon these thy servants, this man and this woman, whom we bless in thy Name; that they, living faithfully together, may surely perform and keep the vow and covenant betwixt them made (whereof this Ring given and received is a token and pledge) and may ever remain in perfect love and peace together, and live according to thy laws; through Jesus Christ our Lord. Amen.

The Minister may add one or both of the following prayers.

O ALMIGHTY God, Creator of mankind, who only art the wellspring of life; Bestow upon these thy servants, if it be thy will, the gift and heritage of children; and grant that they may see their children brought up in thy faith and fear, to the honour and glory of thy Name; through Jesus Christ our Lord. Amen.

O GOD, who hast so consecrated the state of Matrimony that in it is represented the spiritual marriage and unity betwixt Christ and his Church; Look mercifully upon these thy servants, that they may love, honour, and cherish each other, and so live together in faithfulness and patience, in wisdom and true godliness, that their home may be a haven of blessing and of peace; through the same Jesus Christ our Lord, who liveth and reigneth with thee and the Holy Spirit ever, one God, world without end. Amen.

Then shall the Minister join their right hands together, and say,

THOSE whom God hath joined together let no man put asunder.

Then shall the Minister speak unto the company.

FOR AS MUCH AS
. . . .
and . . . .
have consented together in holy wedlock, and have witnessed the same before God and this company, and thereto have given and pledged their troth, each to the other, and have declared the same by giving and receiving a Ring, and by joining hands; I pronounce that they are Man and Wife, In the Name of the Father, and of the Son, and of the Holy Ghost. Amen.

The Man and Wife Kneeling, the Minister shall add this Blessing.

GOD the Father, God the son, God the Holy Ghost, bless, preserve, and keep you; the Lord mercifully with his favour look upon you, and fill you with all spiritual benediction and grace; that ye may so live together in this life, that in the world to come ye may have life everlasting. Amen.

The laws respecting Matrimony, whether by publishing the Banns in Churches, or by Licence, being different in the several States, every Minister is left to the direction of those laws, in every thing that regards the civil contract between the parties.

And when the Banns are published, it shall be in the following form: I publish the Banns of Marriage between N. of ...., and N. of .... If any of you know cause, or just impediment, why these two persons should not be joined together in holy Matrimony, ye are to declare it. This is the first (second *or* third) time of asking.

THE WEDDING RING

The best man is in charge of the wedding ring for the bride unless there is a ring bearer who is carrying the real ring. See Chapter 16 for more details. The best man hands the wedding ring to the groom at the proper moment.

If the ceremony is double ring, the active honor attendant is in charge of the ring for the groom. She hands the ring to the bride at the proper moment in the ceremony. See Chapter 16 for more details.

"WHO GIVETH THIS WOMAN"

In some services when the minister asks "Who giveth this woman to be married to this man?" the bride's father answers "Her Mother and I" instead of "I Do" which is customary. Frequently the bride kisses her father before joining the groom. (The minister is the guide here.)

In Catholic ceremonies, after the bride's father escorts her down the aisle, he joins his wife.

The bride relinquishes her father's arm, gives her bouquet to the maid (or matron) of honor, and gives her right arm to the groom.

THE BRIDE'S VEIL, BOUQUET, AND TRAIN

The active maid (or matron) of honor holds the bride's bouquet during the ceremony. She may also toss back the bride's face or blush veil at the proper time, although many brides prefer to have the groom lift the face veil. She also arranges the bride's train for the recessional.

THE GROOM ASSISTS THE BRIDE

The groom assists the bride up or down any steps that might be at the altar of the church.

THE BRIDAL KISS

Some churches do not allow a kiss after the ceremony; others do. If it is allowed, it then becomes a matter of choice.

THE RECESSIONAL

THE ORGANIST

When the ceremony is completed, the organist starts the recessional music.

ORDER OF THE RECESSIONAL

The bride and the groom lead the recessional. The bride takes the groom's right arm unless the minister specifies otherwise.

THE FLOWER GIRL AND THE RING BEARER

The child attendants may follow the bride and groom, but usually they are not a part of the recessional.

THE HONOR ATTENDANTS

There are several arrangements that might be used for the recessional. The minister knows the correct one to use for his church, and he is the deciding factor here. See Chapter 16.

Optional arrangements

A . . . The honor attendant walks with the best man. Bridesmaids are paired with the ushers.

B . . . If bridesmaids walked in pairs in the processional, they may use this same arrangement for the recessional, flower girl following the bride and groom, maid and/or matron of honor, bridesmaids in pairs, ushers in pairs. The best man leaves with the minister to the vestry.

C . . . If there are two honor attendants, the active honor attendant walks with the best man, the second honor attend-

RECESSIONAL OPTIONAL ARRANGEMENTS

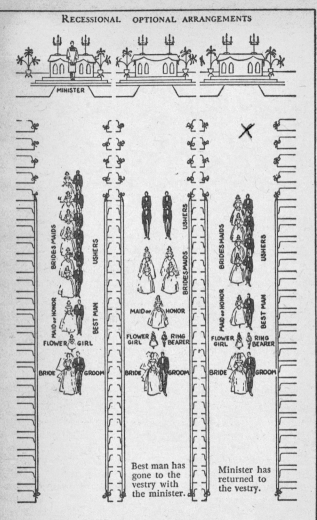

MINISTER

BRIDESMAIDS — USHERS — MAID OF HONOR — BEST MAN — FLOWER GIRL — BRIDE — GROOM

Best man has gone to the vestry with the minister.

BRIDESMAIDS — USHERS — MAID OF HONOR — FLOWER GIRL — RING BEARER — BRIDE — GROOM

Minister has returned to the vestry.

Bride takes the groom's right arm.
In a service wedding maids are usually on the left. The minister's ruling is the deciding one.

ant walks with the head usher, and the bridesmaids follow with the ushers.

THE BRIDESMAIDS

The bridesmaids may walk in pairs or with the ushers.

THE USHERS

Ushers may walk in pairs or with the bridesmaids.

THE BEST MAN

The best man escorts the honor attendant. If there is one more man than maid, the best man follows the minister to the vestry.

THE GUESTS ARE SEATED

If the guests have been standing during the ceremony, they are seated as soon as the entire wedding party reaches the back of the church. They remain seated until after the ushers have returned and escorted the mothers and honor guests.

THE BRIDE'S MOTHER FIRST

The bride's mother is escorted first, usually by the same usher who seated her unless another is chosen for this honor; the bride's father follows.

THE GROOM'S MOTHER NEXT

The groom's mother is next, usually escorted by the same usher who seated her unless another is chosen for this honor; the groom's father follows.

USHERS ESCORT OTHER GUESTS

After the two mothers have been escorted, the ushers escort any other female relatives or guests who are seated in the reserved bride and groom section; male escorts follow.

THE AISLE RIBBONS ARE UNFASTENED

After the female relatives and honored guests who are sitting in the reserved sections are escorted, two ushers remove the aisle ribbons and other guests depart. No other guests are escorted after the aisle ribbons have been removed. See "Aisle Ribbons" in Chapter 16, p. 163.

THE AISLE CARPET

The aisle carpet is not removed.

IF THE CHURCH HAS TWO MAIN AISLES

The one on the left is used for the processional; the one on the right is used for the recessional. If aisle ribbons are being used, both center aisles are ribboned. A small wedding may use the same aisle for both the processional and the recessional.

HOW PARENTS ARE SEATED WHEN THERE ARE TWO MAIN AISLES

The parents are seated in the front row of the center pew, the bride's parents on the left, the groom's on the right. The aisle posts on either side are decorated alike.

If only one aisle is being used for the processional and the recessional, the parents are seated on either side of that aisle. The other aisle is used for seating of guests, and the aisle posts are not necessarily decorated.

RECEPTION AFTERWARDS

If there is to be a reception afterwards and all guests are invited, the wedding party and all guests leave immediately for the place of the reception.

If there is no reception afterwards or the reception only includes the wedding party and a few guests and relatives, the bride and groom, members of the wedding party, and parents stop in the vestibule of the church to greet guests before departing for the place of the reception.

PICTURES AT THE PLACE OF THE RECEPTION

If the reception is immediately following the ceremony and pictures are to be taken, they are taken as soon as the bride and groom and all members of the wedding party arrive at the place of the reception. For this reason the entire wedding party and the parents leave the church as quickly as possible for the place of the reception so that guests are not kept waiting too long before the receiving line can form.

JEWISH CEREMONY

According to Jewish tradition, marriage is a sanctification of life, a consecration of self toward noble ends. It is a spiritual relationship sanctioned by society and sanctified by religion.

The dignity and traditional beauty of the service should be maintained when planning a wedding. A modest wedding should be the choice if the larger one will bring about unnecessary financial strain.

Before setting the date for the marriage ceremony the rabbi must be consulted, because there are many days on which a wedding ceremony may not be scheduled. Many other details should also be discussed before going ahead with wedding plans.

WHEN A MARRIAGE SERVICE MAY BE PERFORMED

The marriage service may be performed on all days except the following: The Sabbath, Festivals, Holy Days and Fast Days, the three-week period beginning with Shivah Asar Be Tammuz (the seventeenth day of the Hebrew month, Tammuz) and ending with Tishah BeAv (the ninth day of the Hebrew month, Av), this period occurring during the summer months.

According to the Committee of Jewish Law and Standards of the Rabbinical Assembly of America, the national organization of Conservative Rabbis, marriages may take place during the days of Sefirah (period between Passover and the Feast of Week) until Lag B'omer, provided the marriage is not accompanied by dancing, singing, or music. Among the Orthodox, customs vary regarding weddings during this period. All groups approve of weddings on Lag B'omer.

THE CHUPAH

The Chupah is the marriage canopy. Rabbis usually insist on the Chupah. It is made of silk or velvet and is sometimes covered with flowers. Often it is suspended from the ceiling.

The Chupah is the symbol of the bridal chamber and denotes the unity of the bridal couple.

The bride, bridegroom, and the rabbi are always under the Chupah during the ceremony. If it is large enough to accommodate them, the parents of both the bride and the bridegroom are also under the Chupah. It is not necessary for any of the attendants to be under it. (Reform rabbis do not always insist upon the Chupah.)

PLACES WHERE THE WEDDING CEREMONY MAY BE HELD

Although weddings may be held anywhere, including hotels and ballrooms, most rabbis prefer weddings in the synagogue, rabbi's study, or at home.

FASTING

The bride and the bridegroom are expected to fast on their wedding day in order to obtain forgiveness for their sins. Fasting is not required if the ceremony follows upon the Holy Day.

ORDER OF THE PROCESSIONAL

There is no order fixed by Jewish Law. Parents of the bride and the bridegroom take part in the processional. The rabbi must be consulted as to his preference of order.

MUSIC

The bride and the bridegroom must confer with the Hazzan (Cantor) of the Congregation on the music for the wedding. Where there is no Hazzan, the rabbi should be consulted.

SEATING

There is usually no concern over the seating of guests. When seats are specified, the Orthodox and Conservative designate the right side for the bride and the left side for the groom. The Reform, however, reserves the right side for the groom's family and the left side for the bride's.

THE SABBATH PRIOR TO THE MARRIAGE

The bride and the bridegroom should attend services in the synagogue on the Sabbath preceding the marriage service. The bridegroom should notify the synagogue officials that he, his family, the bride, and her family will be present.

The bridegroom will be accorded the honor of being called up to the Torah for an "Aliyah."

Following the service, it is the custom for the parents of the groom to provide "Kiddush" for members of the congregation and their guests.

HEADCOVERING

Among the Orthodox and Conservative, but not the Reform, the groom and all other men wear a headcovering, especially if the wedding is held in the synagogue. These will be furnished at the synagogue if attendants do not own them. Top hats are sometimes worn if the wedding is an elaborate one.

The head of the bride is covered. A veil is not required but it is customary for a bride to wear one even if her dress is street length.

Hats are not always required for women guests.

DECORATIONS AND FLOWERS

Decorations are used in keeping with the reverence of the wedding ceremony.

THE RING

The Orthodox and Conservative require the ring to be a plain gold band without gems. During the ceremony it is placed upon the bride's forefinger of her right hand. She may change the ring to the fourth finger, left hand, after the ceremony.

The bride may give the groom a marriage band if she so desires.

In the Reform service the ring is placed on the bride's fourth finger, left hand.

CIVIL MARRIAGE

Although a couple that have been married in a civil ceremony are considered legally married, nevertheless rabbis frown upon it. They feel that only a religious ceremony gives the proper dignity and blessing that is necessary for a permanent union of two people.

This reflects the thinking of all groups.

THE WEDDING CEREMONY

The following wedding service is taken from the *Rabbinical Assembly Manual* (Conservative) published by the Rabbinical Assembly of America and reprinted with their permission.

The Hebrew portions are omitted and only the English translation is included in the following excerpt.

1. Vocal selection.
2. Processional.
3. Blessed may you be who come in the name of the Lord.

    If the ceremony takes place in a Synagogue, add:

    We bless you out of the house of the Lord.
4. May He Who is mighty, blessed and great above all, send His abounding blessings to the bridegroom and the bride.
5. Address or prayer by the Rabbi.
6. Blessing of betrothal.

    The cup of Wine is presented to the Bridegroom and then to the Bride.

7a. *The Rabbi may address the bridegroom:*

    Do you .... take .... to be your lawful wedded wife, to love, to honor and to cherish?

    The Rabbi may then address the bride:

    Do you .... take .... to be your lawful wedded husband, to love, to honor and to cherish?

7b. *The Rabbi instructs the Bridegroom:*

    Then do you .... put this ring upon the finger of your bride and say to her:
        Be thou consecrated unto me, as my wife, by this ring, according to the Law of Moses and of Israel.

    The Rabbi bids the Bride to repeat the following:

    May this ring I receive from thee be a token of my having become thy wife according to the Law of Moses and of Israel.

    If two rings are used, the Bride may say:

    This ring is a symbol that thou art my husband in accordance with the Law of Moses and of Israel.
8. The Kesubah (marriage document) is read.
9. The Seven Benedictions:
        Blessed art Thou, O Lord our God, King of the

universe, who createst the fruit of the vine, symbol of joy.

Blessed art Thou, O Lord our God, King of the universe, who hast created all things to Thy glory.

Blessed art Thou, O Lord our God, King of the universe, Creator of man.

Blessed art Thou, O Lord our God, King of the universe, who hast made man in Thine image, after Thy likeness, and hast prepared unto him, out of his very self, a perpetual fabric of life. Blessed art Thou, O Lord, Creator of man.

Blessed art Thou, O Lord, who makest Zion joyful through these Thy children.

O make these loved companions greatly to rejoice, even as of old Thou didst gladden Thy creatures in the garden of Eden. Blessed art Thou, O Lord, who makest bridegroom and bride rejoice.

Blessed art Thou, O Lord our God, King of the universe, who hast created joy and gladness, the bridegroom and the bride, mirth and exultation, pleasure and delight, love and brotherhood, peace and fellowship.

Blessed art Thou, O Lord, who sendest abounding joy to the bridegroom and the bride.

The cup is again presented to the bridegroom and the bride.

10. *The Rabbi then says:*

By virtue of the authority vested in me as a Rabbi in Israel, I now pronounce you, ... and you .... husband and wife, in conformity with the laws of the State of .... and in accordance with the Laws of Moses and of Israel, and as you bow your heads, I invoke God's blessing upon you.

11. The Lord bless you, and keep you: the Lord make His face to shine upon you, and be gracious unto you. The Lord lift up His countenance upon you, and give you peace. May the Lord implant His spirit within you and grant you length of days, vigor of body, deep and abiding mutual understanding, companionship and love, increasing with the passage of the years and in the fulness of peace. Amen.

12. *The Rabbi then continues, as a glass is placed on the floor:*

> At the conclusion of the traditional marriage service it is customary for the groom to break a glass, in symbolic recognition of the fact that even in the moment of our supreme personal happiness we are not forgetful of the sorrows that have overtaken the house of Israel in the course of the centuries.

When the glass is crushed under foot, all say:

Mazel Tov

13. Recessional

ROMAN CATHOLIC CEREMONY

THE CATHOLIC CEREMONY PREPARATION

Catholics have what is known as the prenuptial investigation of the freedom of the bride and the bridegroom to enter into marriage.

The bride and the bridegroom are interviewed during which time the prenuptial questionnaire is filled out.

If the parties are not well known to the pastor, two affidavits for each are obtained from either the parents, close relatives, or friends, attesting to the freedom of the parties to enter into marriage.

A recent issue of the baptismal certificate is necessary (it must have been reissued not later than six months prior to the date that the marriage takes place).

Copies of the first Holy Communion and Confirmation certificates are required.

The couple must attend six premarriage instructional conferences, which usually last forty-five minutes to one hour each.

A couple contemplating marriage should consult the pastor at least one month before the date of their intended marriage, preferably earlier.

BANNS

The Banns are a public proclamation of an approaching marriage.

The Banns are published in the church bulletin or read

aloud three Sundays prior to the performance of the ceremony.

The Banns are also read in any parishes in which the bride and the bridegroom have lived for a six-month period or longer after the bride has attained the age of twelve and the groom the age of fourteen.

The Banns are announced in order that anyone who knows of an impediment to the marriage may declare it to the pastor of the church.

The Banns are announced only when both parties to the marriage are Catholics.

The Banns can be dispensed with for lack of time or for other sufficient reasons.

WHEN A CATHOLIC CEREMONY MAY NOT TAKE PLACE

The full Catholic ceremony with the Nuptial Mass and the Nuptial Blessing is forbidden during Lent and Advent, because these periods are times of penance.

Catholics may be married in a *simple* ceremony during Lent and Advent.

PLACES WHERE THE WEDDING CEREMONY MAY BE HELD

The Catholic ceremony with The Mass and Nuptial Blessing must be held in the church or chapel.

If the bride and the groom do not belong to the same parish the ceremony should be held in the parish of the bride.

ESSENTIALS NECESSARY FOR VALIDITY

The bare essentials necessary for the validity and lawfulness of the marriage are the performance of the ceremony in the presence of a Catholic priest as well as in the presence of two Catholic witnesses.

ATTENDANTS

Although the two witnesses must be Catholic, other members of the wedding party need not be.

TIME OF THE CEREMONY

A wedding without The Mass may be held in the morning before noon. It is presumed that two Catholics will be married at Mass.

A wedding without The Mass may be held in the morning or in the afternoon.

Ceremonies are not held after six o'clock in the evening.

DECORATIONS

Decorations for the wedding should be in good taste and in accordance with local custom.

MUSIC

Traditional Catholic church music must be used.

FEES

If the soloist is not a friend, a prearranged fee is given. There is usually a set fee for the organist. The choir is not paid. The amount of the voluntary offering given to the church should be in conformity to the amount spent on the overall celebration.

HEADCOVERING

Headcoverings are worn by all the women, both participants and guests.

PROCESSIONAL

The processional follows the standard procedure. The bridegroom and the best man enter from the side door or from the sacristy. The wedding party marches down the center aisle, the bride on the arm of her father coming last. After the bride's father has given her in marriage, he takes his place with the bride's mother on the left side of the church.

RECESSIONAL

The recessional follows the standard procedure.

MIXED MARRIAGES

Nowadays most dioceses permit a marriage of a Catholic and a Protestant (or Jew) in the church. Information on the hours that the ceremony can take place may be secured from the local pastor.

In most dioceses where mixed marriages are permitted in the church, the ceremony is performed before six o'clock in the evening.

In dioceses where mixed marriages are not performed in the church, the ceremony is performed either in the presbytery, the sacristy, or in a private chapel designated for such a marriage.

The marriage is a simple ceremony without the Nuptial Mass.

The Catholic party must have a baptismal certificate.

Besides the filling out of the prenuptial questionnaire, both parties sign promises guaranteeing to baptize and educate in the Catholic faith alone all the children to be born of this marriage.

The non-Catholic further promises that he will not in any way interfere with the Catholic party in the practice of his (or her) religion.

SECOND MARRIAGES (WIDOW OR WIDOWER)

A widow or widower may be married in the church with the Nuptial Mass. If the bride received the Nuptial Blessing at her first marriage she does not receive it again.

CIVIL MARRIAGES

Marriages attempted by Catholics, whether among themselves or with a non-Catholic, before a civil magistrate or minister of another religion are neither valid nor lawful in the eyes of the Catholic church.

Marriages of baptized Protestants contracted in a legal manner before minister or magistrate are regarded as the valid Sacrament of Matrimony by the Catholic church and can be broken only by the death of one of the parties.

DIVORCED MAN OR WOMAN

Civil divorce is not recognized by the Catholic church. Marriage validly entered into between two baptized persons can be broken only by the death of one of the parties.

If a marriage is not properly entered into, the church tribunal considers the case. If it is established that the marriage was invalid from the very beginning the church grants a declaration of nullity.

THE CATHOLIC MARRIAGE CEREMONY

The following Roman Catholic Ceremony is taken from *The Priest's New Ritual,* compiled by The Reverend Paul

Griffith, revised in accord with the latest Vatican Edition of the Roman Edition of the Roman Ritual and published by P. J. Kenedy and Sons.

The priest proceeds to the altar, genuflects and faces the congregation awaiting the entrance of the bridal party. The bridal couple approach him in the presence of two witnesses and perhaps other attendants. Then the priest begins:

(*Kneel*)

Priest:

In the name of the Father and of the Son and of the Holy Ghost. Amen.
Our help is in the name of the Lord.
Who made heaven and earth.
O Lord, hear my prayer.
And let my cry come unto Thee.
The Lord be with you.
And with your spirit.

LET US PRAY

O Lord, we implore Thee, let Thy inspiration precede our actions and Thy help further them, so that all our prayers and all our deeds may ever take their beginning from Thee and, so begun, may through Thee reach completion. Through Christ our Lord. Amen.

INSTRUCTION BEFORE MARRIAGE

My dear friends: You are about to enter into a union which is most sacred and most serious. It is most sacred, because established by God Himself; most serious, because it will bind you together for life in a relationship so close and so intimate, that it will profoundly influence your whole future. That future, with its hopes and disappointments, its successes and its failures, its pleasures and its pains, its joys and its sorrows, is hidden from your eyes. You know that these elements are mingled in every life, and are to be expected in your own. And so not knowing what is before you, you take each other for better or for worse, for richer or for poorer, in sickness and in health, until death.

Truly, then, these words are most serious. It is a beautiful tribute to your undoubted faith in each other, that recognizing their full import, you are nevertheless, so willing and ready to pronounce them. And because these words involve such solemn obligations, it is most fitting that you rest the security of your wedded life upon the great principle of self-sacrifice. And so you begin your married life by the voluntary and complete surrender of your individual lives in the interest of that deeper and wider life which you are to have in common. Henceforth you will belong entirely to each other; you will be one in mind, one in heart, and one in affections. And whatever sacrifices you may hereafter be required to make to preserve this mutual life, always make them generously. Sacrifice is usually difficult and irksome. Only love can make it easy; and perfect love can make it a joy. We are willing to give in proportion as we love. And when love is perfect the sacrifice is complete. God so loved the world that He gave His Only begotten Son; and the Son so loved us that He gave Himself for our salvation. "Greater love than this no man hath, that a man lay down his life for his friends."

No greater blessing can come to your married life than pure conjugal love, loyal and true to the end. May, then, this love with which you join your hands and hearts today, never fail, but grow deeper and stronger as the years go on. And if true love and the unselfish spirit of perfect sacrifice guide your every action, you can expect the greatest measure of earthly happiness that may be allotted to man in this vale of tears. The rest is in the hands of God. Nor will God be wanting to your needs; He will pledge you the life-long support of His graces in the Holy Sacrament which you are now going to receive.

SEALING OF THE MARRIAGE BOND

The priest asks the groom:

N., will you take N., here present, for your lawful wife according to the rite of our holy Mother, the Church?

The groom answers:

I will.

Then the priest asks the bride:

N., will you take N., here present, for your lawful husband according to the rite of our holy Mother, the Church?

The bride answers:

I will.

Then the priest asks the couple to join their right hands and asks them to say after him:

Groom:

I, *N.N.*, take you, *N.N.*, for my lawful wife, to have and to hold, from this day forward, for better, for worse, for richer, for poorer, in sickness and in health, until death do us part.

Bride:

I, *N.N.*, take you, *N.N.*, for my lawful husband, to have and to hold, from this day forward, for better, for worse, for richer, for poorer, in sickness and in health, until death do us part.

CONFIRMATION OF THE MARRIAGE BOND

I join you in matrimony: In the name of the Father and of the Son, and of the Holy Ghost. Amen.

Priest:

I call upon all of you here present to be witnesses of this holy union which I have now blessed. "What God has joined together, let not man put asunder."

The priest blesses them with holy water.

BLESSING OF THE WEDDING RINGS

Our help is in the name of the Lord.
Who made heaven and earth.
O Lord, hear my prayer.
And let my cry come unto Thee.
The Lord be with you.
And with your spirit.

LET US PRAY

Bless, O Lord, these rings, which we are blessing in Thy name, so that they who wear them, keeping faith with each other in unbroken loyalty, may ever remain at peace with Thee, obedient to Thy will, and may live together always in mutual love. Through Christ our Lord. Amen.

Then the priest sprinkles the rings with holy water.

GIVING THE RINGS

Priest:

Now that you have sealed a truly Christian marriage, give these wedding rings to each other, saying after me:

Groom:

In the name of the Father, and of the Son, and of the Holy Spirit. Take and wear this ring as a pledge of my fidelity.

Bride:

In the name of the Father, and of the Son, and of the Holy Spirit. Take and wear this ring as a pledge of my fidelity.

BLESSING
(Psalms 127)

Priest:

Happy are you who fear the Lord, who walk in His ways!

For you shall eat the fruit of your handiwork; happy shall be, and favored.

Your wife shall be like a fruitful vine in the recesses of your home;

Your children like olive plants around your table.

Behold, thus is the man blessed who fears the Lord.

The Lord bless you from Sion: May you see the prosperity of Jerusalem all the days of your life;

May you see your children's children. Peace be upon Israel!

Glory be to the Father, and to the Son, and to the Holy Spirit.

As it was in the beginning, is now, and ever shall be, world without end. Amen.

> Lord, have mercy.
> Christ, have mercy.
> Lord, have mercy.
> Our Father, etc. . . . (*in silence*)
> And lead us not into temptation.
> But deliver us from evil.
> Grant salvation to Thy servants.
> For their hope, O my God, is in Thee.
> Send them aid, O Lord, from Thy holy place.
> And watch over them from Sion.
> O Lord, hear my prayer.
> And let my cry come unto Thee.
> The Lord be with you.
> And with your spirit.

LET US PRAY

Almighty and everlasting God, Who by Thy power didst create Adam and Eve, our first parents, and join them in a holy union, sanctify the hearts and the bodies of these Thy servants, and bless them; and make them one in the union and love of true affection. Through Christ our Lord. Amen.

May Almighty God bless you by the Word of His mouth, and unite your hearts in the enduring bond of pure love. Amen.

May you be blessed in your children, and by the love that you lavish on them be returned a hundredfold. Amen.

Priest:

May the peace of Christ dwell always in your hearts and in your home; may you have true friends to stand by you, both in joy and in sorrow. May you be ready with help and consolation for all those who come to you in need; and may the blessings promised to the compassionate descend in abundance on your house. Amen.

May you be blessed in your work and enjoy its fruits. May cares never cause you distress, nor the desire for earthly possessions lead you astray; but may your hearts' concern be always for the treasures laid up for you in the life in heaven. Amen.

May the Lord grant you fulness of years, so that you may reap the harvest of a good life, and, after you have served Him with loyalty in His kingdom on earth, may He take you up into His eternal dominions in heaven.

Through our Lord Jesus Christ His Son, Who lives and reigns with Him in the unity of the Holy Spirit, God, world without end. Amen.

THE NUPTIAL BLESSING

Let us pray:

O Lord, heed our humble prayers, and in Thy kindness prosper the institution of marriage which Thou has ordained for the propagation of the human race; so that what this morning is joined by Thy authority may be preserved by Thy assistance. Through Christ our Lord. Amen.

Let us pray:

O God, being Almighty, Thou hast created all things out of nothing. First, Thou hast watched over the beginnings of the universe. Then, Thou hast created man to Thy image, and didst appoint a woman to be his constant helpmate. For this reason, Thou hast made woman's body from the flesh of man; at the same time teaching that what Thou hast made of one common source might never lawfully be separated. O God, Thou hast blessed marriage with a mystery so excellent that in the marriage union, Thou hast reflected the union of Christ and the Church. O God, Thou hast given woman to man, and thereby Thou hast given a blessing that neither the punishment for original sin nor the sentence of the flood has diminished. Mercifully behold Thy handmaid, promised in marriage, who prays for Thy protection and strength. May the burden of her marriage be one of peace and love. Faithful and chaste, may her marriage be in Christ. May she ever follow the example of holy women; dear to her husband like Rachel, wise like Rebecca, long-lived and faithful like Sarah. May the author of sin work no evil in her; may she ever keep the faith and the commandments. May she be faithful to her husband and avoid all evil embraces; may she correct any personal weakness with proper discipline.

Let her be serious in conduct, outstanding for her modesty, learned in divine doctrines, fruitful in children. Let her life be good and innocent. Let her come finally to the rest of the blessed in heaven. May they both see their children's children unto the third and fourth generation, thus realizing the old age which they desire. Through the same Lord, Jesus Christ, Thy Son, who liveth and reigneth with Thee, in the unity of the Holy Ghost, God for ever and ever. Amen.

The priest then continues the Mass, saying:

Remove us, we beseech Thee O Lord, from all evils, past, present and future and by the intercession of the blessed and glorious Mary ever Virgin, Mother of God, with Thy blessed Apostles Peter and Paul and Andrew, and all the Saints graciously give peace in our day, that aided by the help of Thy Mercy, we may be always free from sin and secure from all disturbance.

Through the same our Lord Jesus Christ Thy Son, Who liveth and reigneth with Thee in the unity of the Holy Ghost, God.

Priest: World without end.

Server: Amen.

Priest: May the peace of the Lord be always with you.
Server: And with thy spirit.
Priest: May this commingling and consecration of the Body
and Blood of our Lord Jesus Christ avail us who receive it
unto life eternal. Amen.

LET US PRAY

Look down, we beseech Thee, O Lord, upon these Thy
servants, and graciously protect Thy institutions, whereby
Thou hast provided for the propagation of mankind; that
those who are joined together by Thine authority may be
preserved by Thy help. Through Christ our Lord. Amen.

EXHORTATION AFTER MARRIAGE

Having been united in the holy bonds of matrimony,
give thanks to the Almighty for the favors which He has
bestowed upon you. The graces which you have received
have been granted for the purpose of animating you in
the discharge of the obligations which the marriage life im-
poses, and which are beautifully expressed in these words
of the Apostle: "Let women be subject to their husbands,
as to the Lord; for the husband is the head of the wife,
as Christ is the head of the Church. . . .Therefore, as the
Church is subject to Christ, so also let the wives to be
their husbands in all things. Husbands, love your wives,
as Christ also loved the Church, and delivered Himself up
for it, that He might sanctify it, cleansing it by the laver
of water in the word of life. . . . So also ought men to love
their wives as their own bodies." Ever mindful of these
duties which you owe to each other, and to those with
whose welfare you may be especially charged, cherish
with solicitude the grace that has this day been conferred
upon you; it will direct you in every difficulty; it will comfort you in the hour of trial; it will be a continual source
of peace, of joy, of mutual affection on earth, and a pledge
of your eternal and perfect union in heaven.

Go in peace, and may the Lord be with you always.
Amen.

Chapter 22. The Reception

THE FORMAL RECEPTION

INVITATIONS

Engraved invitations are always issued for the formal or ultra-formal reception or breakfast.

PLACE

The reception or breakfast following an ultra-formal or formal wedding may be held at home, in a large room or suite of rooms at a private club or hotel, in the garden, or in the garden or home of a relative or friend. See page 256.

DECORATIONS

For the ultra-formal or formal reception or breakfast, decorators and florists combine their talents to create a proper setting for such an occasion.

RECEIVING LINE

There is always a receiving line at the ultra-formal or formal reception or breakfast. See page 237.

ANNOUNCER

There is always an announcer at the large ultra-formal or formal reception or breakfast. See page 236.

MENU

A reception or breakfast following an ultra-formal or formal wedding is usually very large and lavish, with all details handled by professionals. In large cities bridal services are available to take charge of the arrangements for such a reception. See page 255.

If a bridal service is not available and the reception or breakfast is being held at home, the bride's mother contacts local caterers, florists, and decorators to prepare and serve the food and liquid refreshment, to supply flowers, and to decorate. See page 253.

If the reception is being held at a private club or hotel, the food and liquid refreshment are prepared and served by the staff; decorators are engaged to take over the decorations.

In some cities there are hotels that specialize in wedding receptions. See page 255.

THE BRIDE'S AND PARENTS' TABLES

At ultra-formal or formal receptions, there is usually a bride's table and sometimes a parents' table. See pages 240-242.

WEDDING CAKE

There is always a beautifully decorated wedding cake at the formal or ultra-formal reception and sometimes a groom's cake. See page 243.

MUSIC AND DANCING

Music is an important part of the ultra-formal or formal reception and there is usually dancing. See page 250.

TOASTS

There are always toasts at the ultra-formal or formal reception. See page 249.

FRIENDS TO ASSIST

Friends are invited to assist at the formal or ultra-formal reception. See page 233.

THE WEDDING GUEST BOOK

There is always a wedding guest book at the formal or ultra-formal reception. See page 247.

PICTURES

Pictures are always taken of the bridal party at the ultra-formal or formal reception. See page 252.

THE SEMI-FORMAL RECEPTION

INVITATIONS

Engraved invitations are issued if the reception or breakfast is large. If only a few guests are invited, they may be invited verbally or by handwritten notes. See page 60.

PLACE

The reception or breakfast following a semi-formal wedding may be held at home or in the garden, in a room or suite of rooms at a club or hotel, at a friend's home or garden, in the church parlor or reception room, in a rented hall, or at a private dining room in a restaurant.

DECORATIONS

For the semi-formal reception or breakfast, florists are often assisted in the decorating by members of the family and friends.

RECEIVING LINE

There is usually a receiving line at the semi-formal reception. See the section on "The Receiving Line," p. 236.

ANNOUNCER

There is never a professional announcer at the semi-formal reception. If the guest list is very large, the bride's mother asks a friend to assist with introductions. See page 236.

MENU

The menu may be as varied as for the formal reception and may be prepared and served by professionals. Very often if the reception is being held at home some of the food is prepared by members of the household and the remainder ordered.

For appropriate types of food to serve, see page 244.

For detailed procedure of the method to serve guests, see page 245.

THE BRIDE'S AND PARENTS' TABLES

There is very seldom a bride's or parents' table at the semi-formal reception.

WEDDING CAKE

There is always a beautifully decorated wedding cake at the semi-formal reception or breakfast, and the bride and groom traditionally cut and share the first slice.

MUSIC AND DANCING

Dancing does not usually follow the semi-formal reception. There is ordinarily some sort of music, however, but a piano, an organ, or even a phonograph may suffice.

TOASTS

There are usually toasts at the semi-formal reception. See page 249.

FRIENDS TO ASSIST

Close friends play an important part in the semi-formal reception, helping with the table decorations and the decorations at the place of the reception. Many times friends assist in serving the buffet dishes, serve the punch or coffee, cut the wedding cake, as well as assist in greeting the guests. See page 233.

THE WEDDING GUEST BOOK

A wedding guest book is used at the semi-formal reception or breakfast. See page 247.

PICTURES

Pictures are usually taken at the semi-formal reception or breakfast. See page 252.

THE INFORMAL RECEPTION

INVITATIONS

Engraved invitations are not necessary for the informal reception or breakfast. Friends are more often invited verbally or by handwritten notes. If, however, the reception is to be very large, engraved invitations are often issued.

PLACE

Since the guest list is ordinarily small for the informal wedding, the reception or breakfast held afterwards is usually at home, although it may be held at any convenient place. Many times it is held in the church reception room or in a small private dining room at a club, hotel, or restaurant. Sometimes a large table is reserved at a hotel dining room or restaurant.

DECORATIONS

For the informal reception or breakfast, members of the family or friends frequently do whatever decorating is desired, using a few cut flowers and greenery. Elaborate decorations are out of place at the informal reception or breakfast.

RECEIVING LINE

There is no receiving line at the informal reception or breakfast; after the ceremony the bride and groom turn around and receive the well wishes of their friends and relatives.

MENU

The menu may be ordered ahead of time at a club, hotel, or restaurant by the bride's mother; or guests may order from the dining room menu. If the guests are seated, placecards may be used, or guests may seat themselves informally, the bride always at the right of the groom.

The menu may vary. Sometimes a buffet luncheon or dinner is served, and other times only punch and wedding cake.

For appropriate food to serve, see the section, "Type of Menu to Serve," p. 244.

WEDDING CAKE

There is a wedding cake even at the smallest reception or breakfast, and the bride and groom traditionally cut and share the first slice.

MUSIC

There is usually no special music, but this is entirely optional. If space permits, there may be a piano, organ, or an accordion.

TOASTS

There may be toasts even at the most informal reception or breakfast.

FRIENDS TO ASSIST

If the reception or breakfast is to include a large group of guests, friends are invited to assist. See page 233.

THE WEDDING GUEST BOOK

A wedding guest book may be used.

PICTURES

Taking pictures is entirely optional.

DETERMINING THE NUMBER OF GUESTS

This is probably the most exasperating task the bride's mother will encounter during all the plans and preparation for the wedding and the reception. Although it is very much a breach of etiquette on the part of the invited guest to send no reply to a reception invitation, the number who do not is both surprising and alarming. Some method, therefore, must be devised by which the bride's mother can approximate the number of guests to expect, especially if the reception is to be at home. Many more will appear than the courteous acceptances have indicated.

If a caterer is being used for the home reception, he will assist here. Knowing the number of invited guests, he will know the approximate number for whom to prepare.

If the reception is being held at a club or hotel, the hotel or club dining room manager will assist in determining the number of guests for whom to prepare.

If the bride's mother must try to determine the number of guests, the following are a few suggestions:

Both afternoon and evening receptions held on Saturday and Sunday are well attended.

Evening receptions are well attended.

Receptions held on weekdays preclude the attendance of many men.

Christmas receptions, receptions given by parents who are prominent and/or have extensive family connections, or those involving a celebrity are very well attended. Receptions following unusual weddings (such as full military) are well attended.

Summer receptions are not well attended because many people are away on vacations and because of the heat (unless air-conditioning is known to be at the place of the reception).

For morning or afternoon receptions, Monday through Friday, or those held during vacation months, approximately 50 percent of the invited guests will attend the reception. Such as:

```
*In-town invitations sent ............. 300
 Multiplied by two, as most invitations
    are sent to couples ............... 600
 50 percent of 600 .................. 300
```

For receptions held on Saturday or Sunday afternoon or evening or on weekday evenings approximately 60 percent of the invited guests will attend the reception (or 360).

For receptions at Christmas time, unusual receptions (such as military) or when the parents are very prominent and/or have large family connections, approximately 70 percent of the invited guests will attend the reception (or 420). When a celebrity is being married, or if the wedding is the social highlight of the year, approximately 85 percent of the invited guests will attend the reception (or 510).

WHEN FRIENDS ASSIST AT THE RECEPTION

Whether the reception or breakfast is at home, in the garden, or at a club or hotel where a trained staff prepare and serve the food and liquid refreshment, friends are still needed to assist with the many charming customs attached to a beautiful wedding reception. Few receptions would be successful without such assistance.

Even at the most formal reception friends are asked by the bride's mother to assist, and they are very happy and flattered to be invited to do so. Being asked to cut the wedding cake, serve the punch or coffee, greet the guests, keep the wedding guest book, etc., is a compliment to a friend or relative. These traditional customs take on a more personal note when performed by friends or relatives.

At large receptions many assistants are needed. If the festivities are to continue for two or more hours, one group may be asked to serve for one hour and another group for the next hour, etc.

An assistant list will have to be compiled and a duty and time assigned to each assistant.

---

* All of these percentages are based on in-town invitations issued.

If the reception is somewhere other than at home, before compiling the assistant list, someone should go to the place of the reception and draw a rough sketch of the reception room, marking all entrances and locations of the buffet tables, receiving line, cake table, punch tables, and guest book table. It is now easy to know where to station assistants to the best advantage.

After the assistant list is compiled and a time and duty assigned, each assistant should be WRITTEN and invited to assist at the reception. The assigned duty and time she is to serve are included in the written note. Writing short notes is much easier than trying to reach friends by telephone. The written note gives the assistant a reference to consult just before the reception so she may be certain of her time assignment.

Assistants are written about two weeks before the reception, informals or the fold-over card, with or without the bride's mother's name, being used for this.

A very close friend or relative may be asked to take charge of a duplicate list at the reception. From the duplicate list she can assume the responsibility of making any last-minute changes.

The bride's mother will find that having a definite plan in mind for assistants and their duties is most necessary for the success of a reception, whether it is at home or somewhere else. This plan seems to be the least complicated and will eliminate most mistakes and many telephone calls by and to the bride's mother.

This plan may be used for all receptions when friends are asked to assist:

1...Make a list and a duplicate list of friends who are to assist at the reception.

2...Assign each a duty and a time she is to serve. If the reception is to last several hours, each assistant might serve for one hour.

3...Write a personal note to each assistant inviting her to assist and giving her the assigned duty and time.

4...Ask one special, capable friend or relative to take charge of the duplicate list, bringing it to the reception so that she is responsible for any last minute changes or substitutions.

5...Keep a list handy at home so that any necessary changes can be made before the day of the reception.

Sample of note to assistants:

Dear Mary:

I hope you will be able to assist at Nancy and Larry's reception, Thursday, the tenth of June. Nancy and I would like you to cut and serve the wedding cake from five to six. I hope this fits into your schedule. If not, please let me know so the necessary changes can be made. Aline Abel will be in charge of the assistant list at the reception. We are looking forward to seeing you.

Affectionately,

RESPONSIBILITIES THAT MAY BE ASSIGNED TO FRIENDS WHO ARE ASSISTING

At the home or garden reception

Cutting and serving the wedding cake.

Pouring and serving the coffee, punch, or tea.

Taking charge of the bridal guest book.

Taking charge of the bridal gift book.

Passing sandwiches, canapes, mints, etc.

Supervising the buffet tables.

Assisting in the kitchen if kitchen help is limited.

Greeting guests at each door or entrance to the home or garden.

Designating a place for guests' wraps, unless there is a maid in attendance.

Showing the wedding gifts.

Assisting with decorations, unless professionals are employed for this.

Passing the rice (young girls are usually assigned to do this).

Circulating among the guests and introducing strangers.

Passing the boxed wedding cake if this is being used.

Removing the empty plates and cups after guests have been served.

Introducing the bride's mother to any guest she might not know. See page 236.

And:

If the parents of the groom are from out of town, it would be gracious to assign a friend to see that they become acquainted or are not left uncomfortably alone.

At club or hotel reception

Cutting and serving the wedding cake.

Pouring and serving the punch, coffee, or tea.

Taking charge of the bridal guest book.

Greeting guests at each door or entrance to the reception room.

Circulating among the guests.

Introducing the bride's mother to any guest she might not know.

Passing the rice (young girls are usually assigned to do this).

Passing the boxed wedding cake if this is being used.

Assisting with the decorations, unless professionals are employed for this.

And:

If the parents of the groom are from out of town, it would be gracious to assign a friend to see that they become acquainted or are not left uncomfortably alone.

The Receiving Line

There is always a receiving line at the formal reception or breakfast.

There may be a receiving line at the semi-formal reception or breakfast, but there is never one at the informal.

THE ANNOUNCER

At large formal receptions there is always an announcer to stand at the beginning of the receiving line. He asks the name of each guest who appears and then gives it to the bride's mother so that she can make the necessary introductions. At large receptions it is very necessary to have an announcer, as many invited guests would be unknown to the bride's mother since the guest list would include business associates of both fathers and the groom, the groom's family friends, and many others.

At the semi-formal reception or in less formal communities a friend very often acts as announcer, introducing herself to any guest she does not know and in turn making the introduction to the bride's mother. If the bride's mother knows all the invited guests, an announcer is unnecessary.

THE BEST MAN, USHERS, AND CHILDREN ATTENDANTS

The best man (unless he is also the father of the groom), children attendants, and ushers do not receive.

THE MINISTER

If the minister stands in the receiving line (which happens occasionally), he stands between the bride and her father.

GLOVES

At the formal reception the bride, bridesmaids, and mothers wear their gloves while the receiving line is intact. At the semi-formal reception gloves may be removed or left on. Fathers and the groom remove their gloves to receive.

1. Announcer (see text)
2. Bride's Mother
3. Groom's Father
4. Groom's Mother
5. Bride's Father
6. Bride
7. Groom
8. Maid (or Matron) of Honor

9, 10, 11. Bridesmaids

The bride's father need not receive. The groom's father need not receive, especially if he is well acquainted with most of the guests. See text.

RECEIVING LINE POSITIONS

1...An announcer (optional), see page 236.
2...The bride's mother.
3...The groom's father. (Optional, see text.)
4...The groom's mother.
5...The bride's father. (Optional, see text.)
6...The bride.
7...The groom.
8...The maid or matron of honor.
9...10...11...12...The bridesmaids, in the order they walked in the processional.

THE BRIDE IS GREETED BEFORE THE GROOM

The bride stands on the groom's right and she is always greeted by the guests before the groom. Occasionally, the arrangement of a room is such that a bride must stand on the groom's left in order to be greeted first by the guests; in this case the bride must change her position rather than have the guests greeted first by the groom. If the groom is in uniform, the bride stands on his left unless this arrangement places her in the wrong position to be greeted first.

FATHERS IN THE RECEIVING LINE

The fathers of the bride and groom may decide whether or not they will be a part of the receiving line. If the bride's father does not stand in line, the groom's father then stands next to the bride.

If the groom's father is from out-of-town he usually stands in the receiving line, since he would know few guests at the reception; in this case the bride's father also stands in the receiving line.

DECEASED PARENT OR PARENTS

If the bride's mother is deceased

If the bride's mother is deceased and her father has not remarried, the father takes the mother's place in the receiving line, or he may ask a woman relative to receive with him. Unless the woman relative is a member of the household, the father is the first in line to greet the guests.

If the bride's father is deceased

If the bride's real father is deceased and the mother has remarried, her present husband may receive with her, or he need not be a part of the receiving line (whichever arrangement the bride prefers). A mother who has not remarried takes her position in the line unescorted.

DIVORCED PARENTS

See Chapter 5 on divorced parents.

DOUBLE WEDDING RECEIVING LINE

If the brides are sisters, two receiving lines may be formed at the reception, the mother heading one line, the father heading the other. Or one receiving line may be formed and the following positions used:

1 . . . Mother of the two brides.
2 . . . Mother-in-law of the elder daughter.
3 . . . Father-in-law of the elder daughter.
4 . . . Mother-in-law of the younger daughter.
5 . . . Father-in-law of the younger daughter.
6 . . . The elder bride.
7 . . . Her groom.
8 . . . The younger bride.
9 . . . Her groom.
10 . . . The elder daughter's maid of honor.
11 . . . 12 . . . 13 . . . Elder daughter's bridesmaids.
14 . . . The younger daughter's maid of honor.
15 . . . 16 . . . 17 . . . Younger daughter's bridesmaids.

If the brides' father stands in line, his position is between 5 and 6.

The two maids of honor may stand together, preceding the bridesmaids.

If the brides are not sisters, two separate receiving lines are usually formed with the participants in their usual positions. See the illustration of the receiving line, page 237.

There are usually two bridal tables, unless the bride and the groom have had the same attendants or they have served as each other's honor attendant. See the section on double weddings in Chapter 2, "Types of Weddings."

The Bride's Table

At many ultra-formal or formal receptions there is a bride's table, even when guests are served buffet style. If there is a bride's table, it is always served.

This table (round, square, or oblong) is placed in an interesting part of the reception room or in a separate room.

At this table the bride, the groom, and their attendants are seated. Sometimes a husband or wife of an attendant is also invited to sit at this table, although it is not obligatory to invite them. Now and then the minister and his wife sit at this table if they are young enough to fit into this age group; their places, however, are usually at the parents' table.

The bride and groom and all members of the wedding

party take their places at this table as soon as all guests have passed through the receiving line.

The bride's table is beautifully decorated and placecards are used.

The wedding cake is usually a part of the decoration of the bride's table. When it is time for the dessert to be served, the bride and the groom cut the first slice of wedding cake together.

Champagne is served throughout the meal and toasts are proposed to the bride and groom. See page 249.

Candles may be used if the meal is in the late afternoon or evening. It is not correct to use candles before then. See page 248.

An optional seating arrangement is shown in the diagram of the bride's table.

THE BRIDE'S TABLE

BEST MAN   BRIDE   GROOM   MATRON OR MAID OF HONOR

BRIDESMAID OR MINISTER'S WIFE   USHER OR MINISTER

USHER

BRIDES-MAID   USHER   BRIDES-MAID   USHER   BRIDESMAID

THE PARENTS' TABLE

If there is a bride's table there may also be a parents' table.

At this table are seated the parents of the bride and of the groom, the minister and his wife (unless they are young enough to be seated at the bride's table), relatives, honored guests, and close friends.

If all guests are being served seated, placecards are used at this table and at all other guest tables. If parents and guests are being served buffet style, placecards may be used at this special parents' table, or it may be simply reserved with the proper number of places.

When the service is buffet style, parents as well as guests assigned to this table assist themselves. The bride's table is always served. Other guests not assigned to this special table serve themselves (or are served by waiters standing behind the buffet tables) and then seat themselves at smaller guest tables which have been placed throughout the room. No placecards are used at the smaller guest tables.

See the diagram for seating arrangement for the parents' table, p. 242.

The Bridal and Parents' Table

At the smaller seated reception or breakfast, all members of the wedding party, parents, close relatives, friends, the minister, and his wife are seated at the same table. The bride sits between the groom (on her left) and the best man (on her right) with the maid (or matron) of honor seated on the left of the groom.

Parents, relatives, friends, and other attendants are seated so that men and ladies alternate.

See the diagram for seating arrangement, p. 242.

The Buffet Tables

If a breakfast or reception is held near a mealtime, the buffet tables contain a greater variety of food than if it is being held at coffee, tea, or cocktail time. An early morning wedding is followed by a breakfast that resembles a luncheon or brunch. Following an early afternoon wedding, the menu is more the cocktail or tea-time type. A later afternoon or evening wedding is followed by a supper or cocktail menu. See the section, "Type of Menu to Serve," p. 244.

Upon arrival each guest goes through the receiving line, greeting all the members of the wedding party. Champagne or punch is then served either by waiters or, less formally, from a punch bowl by friends of the bride's mother (or the

PARENTS' TABLE

GUEST GROOM'S BRIDE'S MINISTER GUEST
       FATHER MOTHER

GUEST   GUEST

GUEST   GUEST

GUEST MINISTER'S BRIDE'S GROOMS GUEST
       WIFE   FATHER MOTHER

✓ BRIDE'S AND PARENTS' TABLE
OR REHEARSAL DINNER

BRIDES- BEST BRIDE GROOM MAID OR MATRON USHER
MAID   MAN   OF HONOR

USHER   BRIDES-
                                         MAID

RELATIVES   RELATIVES
OR   OR
FRIENDS   FRIENDS

RELATIVE   FATHER OF
OR FRIEND   GROOM

RELATIVE MINISTER'S FATHER MOTHER MINISTER BRIDE'S
OR FRIEND WIFE   OF BRIDE OF GROOM   MOTHER

groom's mother or the bride) who are assisting at the reception. After stopping to chat with friends, the guest proceeds to the buffet tables.

Small tables may be placed at random in the reception room so that guests may sit while eating if they so desire. These tables are not "set" with china, crystal, and silverware but are of the small cocktail type and may be covered with white cloths and decorated with small bowls of flowers.

The wedding cake is on a large, beautifully decorated table. After the bride and groom have cut the first slice, the wedding cake is cut and served to guests by waiters or, less formally, by friends of the bride's mother (or the groom's mother or the bride) who may be assisting at the reception.

THE WEDDING CAKE

The wedding cake is a *must* at all wedding receptions, no matter how small or informal the reception may be. The bride and the groom traditionally cut and share the first slice of wedding cake even at the most informal reception. The first slice is cut from the outer part of the lowest tier. The bride and groom usually use a decorated cake knife to cut the first slice, the groom placing his right hand over the right hand of the bride as they cut together.

At formal receptions there might be a second cake called the groom's cake. Pieces of this cake are usually boxed in small, white boxes and tied with white satin ribbon. These small boxes are either put at each person's place at the table or given to the guests at the door as they leave the place of the reception.

The groom's cake is dark fruitcake.

Wedding cakes are ordered at the bakery, at specialty shops, from a caterer, or from an individual making a specialty of this type of service.

The size of the wedding cake will vary according to the number of guests invited to the reception. Anyone who specializes in making wedding cakes will know the correct size for a particular reception.

The groom's cake is ordered at the same time as the bride's cake. If this cake is to be boxed, the boxes are selected at this time also. A variety of boxes are usually carried by anyone specializing in this type of cake.

The bride and groom's cake knife is frequently decorated by tying white satin ribbon and flowers to the handle.

If there is a bride's table, the wedding cake may be in the center, or it may be placed upon a smaller table near that of the bride's. When it is time for dessert, the bride and the groom rise (all the gentlemen at the bride's table also rise) to cut and share the first slice of cake. Cake is then served to those at the bride's table and to all the other guests.

If guests are being served buffet style, the wedding cake is on a beautifully decorated buffet table called the wedding cake table. After the bride and the groom cut and share the first slice of cake, the remainder is cut and served by friends (or waiters) who are assisting at the reception.

CUTTING THE WEDDING CAKE

If the wedding cake is to be a main part of the refreshments (for example, when punch, tiny sandwiches, and wedding cake make up the menu), the bride and groom cut and share the first slice of wedding cake BEFORE the receiving line forms, so that no guest is kept waiting to be served.

If a larger menu is planned and served buffet style and the wedding cake is to be served with the dessert, the bride and groom may wait until all of the guests have gone through the receiving line before cutting and sharing the first slice of wedding cake.

If there is a "bride's table" and other guests are being served buffet style, or if all guests are served seated, the bride and the groom cut and share the first slice of wedding cake with the dessert course. Pieces of wedding cake are then served to the members of the wedding party and guests.

TYPE OF MENU TO SERVE

The festivity following a ceremony held before one o'clock is called a "breakfast."

The festivity following a ceremony held after one o'clock is called a "reception."

A breakfast follows the early-morning ceremony and should be a substantial meal. Since most early-morning weddings follow the Nuptial Mass, the bride and her attendants would have gone without breakfast.

A breakfast held after a later-morning wedding should consist of the type of food served at a morning coffee.

If the ceremony is held near noon, the food at the breakfast is the same kind as that served at a dainty luncheon.

If the ceremony is held in the early afternoon, the reception food is the same kind as that served at an afternoon tea.

A late-afternoon ceremony is followed by a reception with cocktail, dinner, or cocktail-and-dinner-type food served, and may include both hot and cold dishes.

If the ceremony is held after dinner, cocktail food is served at the reception.

Wine, champagne, punch (alcoholic or nonalcoholic), cocktails, or highballs may be served at any breakfast or reception; and a toast to the bride should be given even if it is done with gingerale.

A wedding cake is a *must* and is always present at any wedding breakfast or reception.

METHODS OF SERVING AT THE RECEPTION

1...All seated.
2...All buffet style.
3...Guests buffet style with a bride's table and sometimes a parents' table. See pages 239-240.

PROCEDURE

1...When all are served seated

As soon as the ceremony is over, the bridal party, parents, relatives, and guests invited to the reception leave for the place of the reception.

The bridal party arrives at the place of the reception.

Pictures are taken of the bridal party. See page 252.

The receiving line is formed.

Guests arrive at the place of the reception and go through the receiving line.

If a wedding guest book is being used, guests sign their names either before or after going through the receiving line.

Cocktails, punch, champagne, mixed drinks, or nonalcoholic punch is served while the receiving line is intact.

As soon as the last guest is greeted in the receiving line, the bride and groom lead the way to their tables; parents, relatives, and guests take their places at other tables.

The meal is served, usually with more wine, champagne, etc.

Toasts are proposed, the first one by the best man; others follow.

The bride and groom cut and eat the first slice of wedding cake. See page 243.

If there is dancing, the bride and groom have the first dance together. See page 250.

The bride throws her bridal bouquet.

The bride and groom dress for the wedding trip.

Goodbyes are said to parents and friends.

2...All buffet style

As soon as the ceremony is over, the bridal party, parents, relatives, and invited friends leave for the place of the reception.

The wedding party arrives at the place of the reception.

Pictures are taken of the wedding party. See page 252.

The wedding cake is cut by the bride and the groom.

The receiving line is formed.

Guests arrive at the place of the reception and go through the receiving line.

If a wedding guest book is being used, guests sign their names either before or after going through the receiving line.

Champagne or alcoholic or nonalcoholic punch is served from punch bowls; cocktails or highballs are passed by waiters. Food is served from a buffet table, guests either helping themselves or being served by waiters standing behind the tables. Friends very often cut and serve the wedding cake and punch.

Toasts are offered to the bride and groom.

If there is dancing, the bride and groom have the first dance together. See page 250.

The bride throws her bridal bouquet.

The bride and groom dress for the wedding trip.

Goodbyes are said to parents and friends.

3...When guests are served buffet style and there is a bridal table and sometimes a parents' table

This method of serving is used for the large ultra-formal or formal reception and occasionally for the semi-formal reception. It is never used for the informal reception.

As soon as the ceremony is over, the bridal party, parents, relatives, and invited guests leave for the place of the reception.

Pictures are taken of the bridal party. See page 252.

The receiving line is formed.

Guests arrive at the place of the reception and go through the receiving line.

If a wedding guest book is being used, guests sign their names either before or after going through the receiving line.

Champagne or alcoholic or nonalcoholic punch is served from punch bowls; cocktails or highballs are passed by waiters while the receiving line is intact.

As soon as the last guest is greeted in the receiving line, the bride and groom and the attendants take their places at their table. If there is a parents' table, they take their places at their table. If guests are served buffet style and then eat standing, there is no special table for the parents. If guests are served buffet style and then seat themselves informally at small tables to eat, there is very often a special parents' table. See pages 239-240.

Toasts are made to the bride and groom.

When it is time for the dessert to be served, the bride and groom cut and eat the first slice of wedding cake together. (See the section on "The Wedding Cake," p. 243.) Portions of cake are then served to other members of the bridal party and guests.

If there is dancing, the bride and groom have the first dance together. See page 250.

The bride throws her bridal bouquet.

Goodbyes are said to parents and guests.

PLACECARDS

Placecards can be purchased at the bridal gift consultant shop, gift shops, some department stores, specialty shops, the stationers, and at many other stores.

Placecards are always used on the bride's table at formal receptions. Placecards are always used at a formal seated meal.

THE WEDDING GUEST BOOK

A permanent record of all who attended the wedding reception or breakfast is secured by using a wedding guest book.

This is a decorative book with lined pages for guests' signatures. These books can be purchased at the bridal gift consultant shop, from a bridal service shop, gift stores, many department stores, or the stationers.

The wedding guest book is placed upon a small table at a convenient spot in the reception room, either at the beginning or at the end of the receiving line. Guests may sign in this book either before or after going through the receiving line.

Sometimes the best man is stationed near this book to remind guests to sign, but more often two friends of the bride sit at this table and encourage the guests to sign.

This table is covered with a lovely tablecloth and may also contain the bridal or memory candle.

THE BRIDAL OR MEMORY CANDLE

The bridal or memory candle is a very large candle, usually white and decorated. It is placed upon the wedding guest book table at the reception. This candle may be purchased at a bridal gift consultant shop, a candle store, some department stores, or through a bridal service.

This lovely candle will burn for many hours and is meant to be kept by the bride and the groom and lighted every anniversary.

BRIDAL NAPKINS, MATCH FOLDERS, AND OTHER DECORATIVE EFFECTS

Bridal napkins, match folders, and other decorative bridal effects may be ordered from the bridal gift consultant shop, gift shops, or some department stores and specialty stores.

If these articles are to be monogrammed, they must be ordered many weeks in advance of the wedding.

CANDLES

Candles for decorations may be used for the late afternoon or evening reception, but they are not used for the early-afternoon or morning breakfast.

Decorated candles may be purchased at a bridal gift shop, gift shops, some department stores, or specialty shops. Candles may also be decorated by the caterer or at the bakery where the wedding cake is decorated.

THE MARRIAGE CUP

The use of the marriage cup at the bride's table is an old-world tradition. The bride and groom drink and in so doing plight their troth. This precedes all toasts at the reception.

There are two styles of the marriage cup. The Nuremberg type, which is usually silver (sterling or plated), is made in the shape of a young girl with a large skirt, holding a cup over her head. The cup is on a swivel so that both the bride and the groom may drink from this cup at the same time.

The second type is French and is made in the shape of a small bowl on a pedestal; if this cup is used, the bride drinks first and then the groom.

RICE, RICE BAGS, AND CONFETTI

If rice is being used, a small amount is very often put into tiny plastic bags or bags made of squares of pastel net tied with satin ribbon. Flowers may be added to give a prettier effect. These tiny rice bags are given to each guest just before the bridal pair leaves the place of the reception. They are usually passed to the guests by two or three young girls who are friends or relatives of the bride or groom.

If rice is being thrown, it should be thrown outside the building and (a word of warning) should be tossed gently.

Rose petals or confetti are often used instead of rice.

TOSSING THE BRIDAL BOUQUET

After the bride and groom have finished the wedding repast and before they change into their going-away clothes, the bride throws her bridal bouquet in the traditional manner to her assembled bridesmaids.

TOSSING THE GARTER*

After tossing her bridal bouquet, the bride removes her special blue garter and gives it to the groom. He then tosses it to his ushers and bachelor friends.

TOASTS

The father of the bride proposes the first toast to his daughter and his future son-in-law at the engagement party.

---

* The custom of "tossing the garter" is not used in many locations.

The host or the father of the groom proposes the first toast to the bride and groom at the rehearsal party.

The best man proposes the first toast to the bride and groom at the wedding reception.

If the bride and the groom are seated when toasts are proposed to them, they remain seated even when others stand. After guests have responded to the toast, the bride and groom drink their wine.

Music

There is nearly always music at the ultra-formal or formal reception. Sometimes an orchestra, string quartette, or trio may be employed.

Music may be a part of the semi-formal or informal reception. A string quartette or trio, piano, accordion, organ, or phonograph is sometimes used, although music is entirely optional.

Dancing

Dancing may follow the late-afternoon or evening formal or semi-formal reception.

When the music starts, the groom dances once around the room with his bride, without other guests dancing. The groom then dances with his mother and the bride with her father. Next the groom dances with the bride's mother while the bride dances with the groom's father.

Attendants and guests join in the dancing as the bride's father dances with the groom's mother and the father of the groom dances with the bride's mother.

Hats

Hats or some kind of head covering is required in most churches. Hats need not be worn by lady guests to a home or garden wedding or reception.

Wraps

If the reception is at home, guests' wraps are usually placed upon the beds or furniture of one or two of the bedrooms, either with or without a maid in attendance.

If the reception is at a club or hotel, there should be attendants to take care of ladies' and men's wraps.

THE DOORMAN

At the large home or garden reception, there should be a doorman (especially necessary in case of rain). Most clubs and hotels furnish their own doormen.

UMBRELLAS

If large umbrellas are needed, they may be borrowed from a few golfing friends.

PARKING AT THE RECEPTION

If the reception is large and at home, there is sometimes quite a problem with the parking of guests' cars.

In many large cities there are parking services available where experienced men will park cars as they arrive, returning them when a guest is ready to leave.

In smaller, less-congested communities there are generally parking facilities available nearby, but there should be attendants on hand to park cars and to return them when guests are ready to depart.

If the reception is at a club or hotel, there is usually a large parking area conveniently located. Cars are parked by the guests themselves or by the club or hotel attendants.

It is very important that the parking of guest cars is well planned in advance of the reception.

THE WEATHER WORRY

If the number of friends invited to a home reception is great enough to necessitate the added area of the garden, a canopy should be installed. Canopies can be rented from special bridal agencies or awning shops. In smaller communities they are rented from the funeral director.

In case of cool weather, heaters can be installed in the garden.

SERVING OR NOT SERVING ALCOHOLIC BEVERAGES

Champagne is practically always served at the formal reception, but the serving of alcoholic beverages of any

kind at any type wedding reception or prewedding party
is a matter of personal choice.

Many people feel that alcohol has no place at an occasion
as sacred as marriage, nor do they approve of the younger
people being served that type of refreshment. The decision
of serving alcoholic refreshments is not a matter of finances
but is entirely a matter of personal preference and opinion.

Removing Furniture

At the home reception a few of the larger pieces of furniture may have to be removed if so many guests have been
invited that the house will look crowded. So much should
not be removed that the house looks completely unfurnished.

Taking Pictures at the Reception

Taking pictures of the bridal party is a very necessary part
of the wedding festivities. Since pictures cannot be taken of
the entire wedding party until after the ceremony, they must
be taken after the bridal party arrives at the place of the
reception. This creates a problem if the reception is "immediately following ceremony," as guests are kept waiting at
the door because the receiving line cannot form until after
the photographers have finished. There are two solutions to
this problem.

First: When the reception invitations are being ordered,
instead of having the reception "immediately following ceremony" a time is given in the invitation which allows at least
one hour after the scheduled ceremony time (more if the
city is very large and the place of the reception at a distance) for taking pictures, arranging the receiving line, etc.
If this is done, guests are received as soon as they arrive at
the place of the reception.

Second: For the large semi-formal reception, if the time
of the reception is given "immediately following ceremony,"
arriving guests are invited to come into the reception room
and watch the pictures being made of the wedding party.
As soon as the photographers have finished, the receiving
line forms and guests go through the line.

If this second solution is used, a friend (or two) stands
at the door inviting guests to come in and to go through the
receiving line later, after the photographers have finished.

Guests do not seek refreshments until after they have gone through the receiving line.

The Catering Service

If the reception or breakfast is being held at home or at a club or large reception room where serving facilities and personnel are not adequate to take care of a large reception, the best plan is to engage a caterer's services. This is not necessary if a bridal service has complete charge of the wedding and reception.

Caterers charge by the number of guests served for food, and usually by the cork for any wine, mixed drinks, or champagne.

A catering service will furnish any or all food, the wedding cake, and any or all liquid refreshments, as well as the necessary personnel to set the tables and to serve the food and drink.

Many will supply all china, linen, glasses, silver, punch bowls and cups, ash trays, silver serving trays and bowls, candlesticks, placecards, etc. Some catering services are prepared to supply any extra tables and chairs that might be needed.

The food is usually prepared at their place of business and delivered in time to be served. If it is desired to have the food prepared at home, they will supply cooks, chefs, waiters, waitresses, and bartenders.

Large catering services can also supply the canopy, the aisle carpet for church or home, and an organist with a portable organ.

A catering service is almost a MUST if the reception is very large or if it is being held at home or at some other place where trained personnel is not available.

If a catering service is being used, the date and time must be reserved and the caterers engaged before ordering the reception invitations.

The Bridal Consultant

Most department stores or specialty shops selling wedding gowns and wedding trousseaus have one or more paid employees in the bridal department called bridal consultants.

These bridal consultants will assist the bride, her attendants, and the mothers in choosing the correct costumes for their particular type wedding and will supervise all fittings. They will also give advice as to the correct attire for the groom, his attendants, and the fathers.

Most stores send a representative to the wedding rehearsal and to the ceremony to assist the minister with the spacing of bridesmaids or with any other details of the processional or recessional that he desires.

Some of these stores combine their trousseau and gift departments so that the bride can make her selections of china, silver, and crystal patterns in one store and at one time. A record is kept of the bride's selections so that there is little chance of duplication.

These services are all without additional charge and are invaluable to the bride and her mother.

The Bridal Gift Consultant

In many communities there are specialty shops called bridal gift consultant stores. Frequently large department stores or jewelry stores have a bridal gift consultant department.

The services offered by these shops or departments are so numerous and valuable to a bride that few communities are without them.

Their services are without additional cost if a bride makes her selection of china, crystal, or silver patterns at these shops.

They carry a large line of all types of invitations and announcements, and they will advise the bride and her mother as to the correct type, wording, and manner of addressing them. They keep a record of all the bride's pattern selections and see that no duplications are made.

A representative very often will assist in arranging the gifts at the bride's home, and many shops will furnish plate and tray racks, sometimes the gift table drape, and some will even supply the gift display tables.

For the reception some shops of this kind will supply punch bowls and cups, silver trays, platters, and candle holders, and many will furnish a silver tea or coffee service.

It is a wise bride who makes her gift selections at one of these shops; their courteous advice is correct, efficient, and invaluable.

SPECIAL HOTEL SERVICE

In some cities, if a reception is being held at a hotel that solicits wedding receptions, their social manager will help to select the menu, supervise the preparations of the food and drink, arrange for the decorations and the music, take charge of any seating arrangements, and order the correct size wedding cake. Rooms also are provided in which the bride and groom may change attire before they depart.

There is usually no extra charge for the social manager's services. Although a hotel reception with this kind of supervision is more expensive per person than a home reception, the responsibility is much less. If the bride's family can afford it, they can be assured that the reception will be managed perfectly.

BRIDAL SERVICE

In many large cities and in some smaller communities there are independent firms called "bridal services" who will take over every detail of a wedding and a reception.

They will order, address, stamp, and mail the invitations and announcements. They will supervise the selecting of costumes for the bride, her attendants, and the groom and his attendants, as well as for the mothers and any other members of the wedding party.

They will select or help to select the menu for the reception, make all arrangements with the caterer, and engage the florist and the decorators for the bridal flowers and decorations at the church and at the place of the reception.

One of their bridal consultants will attend the rehearsal and the ceremony and assist the minister with any last-minute details. They will furnish cars for the wedding party and guests and supply any other bridal effects that are needed at the church or at the place of the reception.

Although this type of service is usually quite expensive, the bride's mother might find it is needed for the very large wedding and/or reception. If a bride's mother is deceased this service is often used.

Frequently a bridal service will take over part of a wedding such as only the reception, only the ceremony, or only the invitations; and some firms are interested in the smaller and less lavish weddings.

HOME AND GARDEN CEREMONY AND RECEPTION

GREETING THE GUESTS

At the formal or semi-formal wedding the bride's mother greets the guests as they arrive. If the bride's mother is not living, the bride's father greets them, or if there is an older female relative living in the home such as grandmother or aunt, she takes the place of the mother and greets the guests with the father. If the bride's mother is deceased, the father has not remarried, and there is no older female relative living in the home, the father may ask a female relative or friend to greet the guests with him. The father is the first in line, however. If the bride's mother is deceased and the father has remarried, his present wife greets the guests with him.

If the bride's mother and father are divorced, the father is giving the reception, and the father has not remarried, the bride's mother may receive the guests with him even if the mother has remarried. Since he is the host, the father is the first in line to greet the guests.

At the informal home or garden wedding the guests are greeted by the bride, the groom, and the bride's mother (or father if the mother is deceased). See page 236.

ARRANGING THE ALTAR

An altar is arranged in front of the fireplace, between two windows, or at some other interesting location in the room.

SEATS

If space permits, seats may be provided; otherwise, guests stand during the ceremony. A few seats are provided for any elderly guests.

AISLE RIBBONS AND AISLE CARPET

Ribbons may be put into place to provide an entrance. An aisle carpet is not usually used in the home.

WRAPS

Some arrangement is planned for guests' wraps. A maid or one or two friends may assist here.

PARKING AND DOORMAN

If guests are numerous, a definite plan should be made for the parking of cars.

A doorman will be needed if the guest list is large. He should be provided with a large umbrella.

SUPPLIES NEEDED FOR HOME CEREMONY AND RECEPTION

See list later in this chapter.

ASSISTANTS NEEDED FOR HOME RECEPTION

See page 233.

PREPARING THE GARDEN

If the wedding takes place in the garden, an improvised altar is arranged at the loveliest location. At formal weddings a bridal carpet is used and aisle ribbons are put into place. Seats are usually provided.

The formal garden wedding and/or reception takes endless hours of planning; and the bride's mother needs professional assistance, including nurserymen, decorators, caterers, etc.

The aisle carpet and ribbons are not used at the semiformal or informal garden wedding. If guests are numerous, seats may be provided.

The informal or semi-formal home or garden wedding and reception can be planned perfectly by the bride's mother with the willing assistance of friends, relatives, the minister, and the bride's own family.

HOME AND GARDEN CEREMONY PROCEDURE

FORMAL

If seats have been provided, ushers seat guests as they arrive.

If aisle ribbons are being used, they are now put into place.

A few minutes before the ceremony is ready to begin, the groom's mother takes her place (on the right side, either seated or standing), escorted by an usher; the father follows a few steps behind.

When it is time for the ceremony to start, the bride's

mother takes her place (on the left side, either seated or standing), escorted by an usher.

If there is an aisle carpet, it is now unrolled.

Musicians (or an organist) start the wedding march, which is the signal for the processional to begin.

The minister enters, followed by the groom and best man. All face the center aisle. They may enter from a side door or walk down the aisle if there is no side door.

The ushers are next, walking in pairs.

The bridesmaids follow, either in pairs or singly, then the maid (or matron) of honor, the flower girl, the bride and her father.

If the bride comes down a stairway, her father meets her at the foot of the stairs, where he offers his right arm and escorts her to the altar.

Family and guests stand during the ceremony.

For more detailed description see Chapter 21, "The Church Ceremony."

SEMI-FORMAL

At the semi-formal home ceremony ushers do not seat guests or parents, although seats may be provided if space permits.

Ceremony procedure is the same as for the formal wedding. Music may be used.

INFORMAL

At the informal wedding there is no processional. The bride and groom, already present in the room, step forward when the minister is ready to start the ceremony. Guests and family stand during the ceremony.

THE RECESSIONAL

There is no recessional at the home or garden wedding. If there is to be a receiving line formed in another room, the bride and groom, their parents, and the bride's attendants proceed to that room and receive the guests.

If there is no receiving line, the bride and groom turn around after the ceremony and receive the good wishes of their friends.

ITEMS TO ORDER IN ADVANCE FOR HOME OR GARDEN CEREMONY

FORMAL

Aisle carpet. (If in the garden.)
Aisle ribbons or rope.
Marquee or canopy. (Optional.)
An improvised altar or any special tables or stands the minister might need. (Consult the minister.)
Kneeling cushion or bench. (Consult the minister.)
Extra chairs.

SEMI-FORMAL

A marquee or canopy. (Optional.)
An improvised altar or any special tables or stands the minister might need. (Consult the minister.)
Extra chairs.
A kneeling cushion or bench. (Consult the minister.)

INFORMAL

None of these supplies are needed at the informal ceremony.

ITEMS TO ORDER IN ADVANCE FOR HOME OR GARDEN RECEPTION

The bride's wedding cake.
The groom's wedding cake and boxes.
The bridal napkins.
The wedding candles.
Any monogrammed or decorated match folders or other bridal effects.
The bridal or memory candle.
The marriage cup.
Extra tables and chairs.
Placecards.
The menu, if using a caterer.
Flowers for decorating, if family and friends are assisting with decorations.
The decorating plan, if professionals are being used.
A canopy or tent, if garden is being used.
All food and liquid refreshment, if not using a caterer.
Extra table appointments, if not using a caterer.

ITEMS THAT MAY ALSO BE NEEDED FOR HOME OR GARDEN RECEPTION

The bride's guest book.

A decorated cake knife.

Rice, rose petals, or confetti.

Umbrellas, in case of rain.

Extra coat hangers.

Extra linen, china, flat silver, serving dishes, trays, candle holders, flower bowls and holders, punch cups, ladles and bowls, highball or cocktail glasses, tea or coffee service. (All these articles are usually supplied by a caterer, if one is being used.)

Cigarettes and ash trays.

Corsages for hostesses assisting at the reception.

Ice.

PROFESSIONALS WHO MAY BE NEEDED AT HOME OR GARDEN RECEPTION

Decorator, florist, nurseryman.

The caterer.

Musician.

The photographer.

Domestic help.

Bartender.

Doorman.

A guard for the wedding presents.

Someone to park cars.

A maid to take care of wraps.

An announcer.

EXTRA APPOINTMENTS

Extra linen, china, flat silver, serving dishes, trays, candle holders, flower bowls, punch cups, ladles and bowls, highball or cocktail glasses, and tea or coffee service are usually supplied by the caterer, if one is being used.

If a caterer is not being used, most of the above items can be rented from a bridal rental service. If there is no such service in your city, many of these items may be supplied by the bridal gift consultant shop. If they do not supply them, they will be able to give information as to where they may be obtained.

If a caterer is not being used and none of the above sources is available, extra appointments may be borrowed from friends or a women's club.

Bridal rental services are listed in the yellow pages of the telephone book.

Extra Tables and Chairs

Extra tables and chairs may be rented or borrowed from a rental agency, church, club, or funeral director.

Club or Hotel Reception

Many of the articles listed above will be needed for the club or hotel reception.

Suitable places must be arranged in advance for the bride and groom to change their clothes.

The wedding cake is ordered sent to the club or hotel (unless it is being furnished by them) before the time of the reception.

Flowers for the decorations are also ordered sent there, unless decorators are handling this.

On the day of the reception, the following supplies should be sent or taken to the club or hotel:

Decorated candles, cake knife, bride's guest book and fountain pen, bridal napkins, cigarettes and matches, memory candle, marriage cup, candle holders, necessary extra silver trays, serving dishes, tablecloths, silver tea or coffee service, punch bowl, ladle, small packages of rice or confetti, AND the bride's and groom's going-away clothes.

Chapter 23. Tipping

The newly married couple assumes a different financial status than the young single person, who, during most of the past years, has traveled with parents.

With marriage comes a new conformity to the custom of payment for service, which is commonly referred to as "tipping."

This brief and general guide might prove useful to the bride and groom starting on a honeymoon trip.

A manager or owner of an establishment is not tipped. An employee who gives personal service is supposed to be tipped. Airline employees or employees of private clubs are not tipped. No one is tipped where there is a sign saying "no tipping." Tipping amounts are quite standard, and although it is gracious to tip a little over the minimum, to overtip lavishly is unfair to others and is in bad taste.

In the Home

Maid—One to two weeks' pay at Christmas.

Milkman, paper boy, laundryman, grocery boy—Two to five dollars at Christmas.

Delivery boy—Ten to twenty-five cents for drugstore or telegraph delivery. No tip for department store delivery.

Guest in a Home

Maid or any servant—One dollar for overnight stay. Five dollars for several days' stay.

APARTMENT

Maid, delivery boys—The same as in the home.

Parking lot attendant—Two to five dollars at Christmas.

Elevator man, doorman, porter, superintendent, handy-man—Two percent or 2½ percent of one's annual rent, divided equally at Christmas.

GUEST OF APARTMENT TENANT

Porter or elevator man—For assistance with luggage, fifty cents. More if luggage is very heavy.

Doorman—Twenty-five cents each time he assists.

Maid—Same as for guest in the home.

HOTEL

Doorman—Twenty-five cents for summoning a cab. Fifty cents to one dollar for special services such as assisting during rain or similar courtesies.

Parking attendant—Twenty-five cents for parking car. Twenty-five cents for returning car.

Bellhop—Twenty-five to fifty cents if luggage can be handled in one trip. If more than one trip is required or luggage is heavy, the tip is advanced accordingly. Ten to twenty-five cents for the delivery of a small package.

Room waiter—Twenty-five cents for a small order such as a pot of coffee. Fifteen percent of the total food bill for larger orders. Never less than twenty-five cents, however.

Page—Ten to fifteen cents. If hotel is large and necessitates the coverage of many corridors, the tip is increased.

Porter—Fifty cents for taking a heavy trunk to a room. Fifty cents to two dollars for any difficult special service.

Chambermaid—Twenty-five to fifty cents for an overnight stay. For a week's stay, one dollar.

Valet—No tip unless a very special service has been requested of him.

Elevator starter—No tip for an overnight stay. Twenty-five to fifty cents for a week's stay.

Dining room waiters—See the next section.

RESTAURANT, BAR, OR NIGHTCLUB

Headwaiter—One to five dollars for special service. Nothing for seating and supplying menu.

Waiter or waitress—Fifteen to twenty percent of the total food bill.

Busboy—Is not tipped.

Wine steward—Ten percent of the total amount of the wine check if special services were requested.

Bartender—Ten to fifteen percent of the total amount of the bar bill.

Cigarette girl—Ten to fifteen cents extra for a package of cigarettes.

Hat check girl—Fifteen to twenty-five cents.

Rest room attendant—Ten to twenty-five cents if a special service has been requested. Nothing otherwise.

Parking attendant—Twenty-five cents for parking the car. Twenty-five cents for returning the car.

Train

Pullman porter—Twenty-five cents for a day trip. Fifty cents to one dollar for a night in a berth or roomette. One dollar for a night in a compartment or bedroom. One dollar and fifty cents for a night in a drawing room.

Porter—Twenty-five cents for a day trip. More if special services have been requested.

Dining room waiter—Fifteen to twenty percent of the total food bill.

Room service—Twenty-five cents for pot of coffee. Fifteen to twenty percent of the total food bill for larger orders; never less than twenty-five cents, however.

Station porter—Most stations have a set price of twenty-five to thirty-five cents a bag.

Taxi

Under fifty cents, the tip is ten cents.

Fifty cents to one dollar, the tip is twenty cents.

One to two dollars, the tip is twenty-five cents.

Two to three dollars, the tip is thirty-five to forty cents.

Three to five dollars, the tip is sixty-five to seventy-five cents.

Five to eight dollars, the tip is one dollar.

Eight to ten dollars, the tip is one dollar and fifty cents.

SHIP

The rule is to allow ten percent of the ticket cost for tipping, to be distributed as follows:

Stewardess—Ten percent.
Cabin steward—Thirty percent.
Dining room steward—Thirty percent.
Deck steward—Fifteen to twenty percent.
Bath steward—Ten percent.

OTHER SERVICES ON SHIP

Bartender—Fifteen to twenty percent of the drink check.
Wine steward—Ten percent of the wine check.
Cabin waiter—Fifteen to twenty percent of the wine check.
Bellhop—Fifteen to twenty-five cents.

PLANE

No member of a plane's personnel is ever tipped.
A baggage porter may be tipped twenty-five cents if he has assisted in finding lost luggage or has carried luggage to or from a waiting car.
Airport Porter—The same as a railroad station porter.

INDEX

DO IT!
ALL BY YOURSELF!

☐ GETTING INTO WINE   (8876 • $1.95)

☐ THE ART OF MIXING DRINKS   (8578 • $1.25)

☐ THE MOTHER EARTH NEWS
   HANDBOOK OF HOMEMADE POWER   (8535 • $1.95)

☐ SUPERMARKET SURVIVAL MANUAL   (8233 • $1.25)

☐ AMY VANDERBILT'S EVERYDAY
   ETIQUETTE   (8092 • $1.95)

☐ SOULE'S DICTIONARY OF ENGLISH
   SYNONYMS   (7883 • $1.25)

☐ THE RUTH STOUT NO-WORK
   GARDEN BOOK   (7763 • $1.25)

☐ TREASURY OF CRAFT DESIGN   (7683 • $1.95)

☐ CONSUMER BEWARE   (7484 • $1.95)

☐ BETTER HOMES AND GARDENS
   HANDYMAN BOOK   (6460 • $1.50)

☐ HOW TO BUY STOCKS   (2734 • $1.50)

☐ THE BANTAM BOOK OF CORRECT
   LETTER WRITING   (2203 • $1.25)

☐ THE DRIVER'S HANDBOOK   (2105 • $2.25)

Buy them at your local bookstore or use this handy coupon for ordering: